THERE'S MORE TO
Life
THAN THIS

THERE'S MORE TO *Life* THAN THIS

Healing Messages, Remarkable Stories,
and Insight About the Other Side from

the
LONG ISLAND MEDIUM

THERESA CAPUTO

with

Kristina Grish

ATRIA BOOKS

New York London Toronto Sydney New Delhi

The author would like to thank the following people for permission to share their stories: Pat, beginning on p. 15; Regina, p. 44; Jacqueline, p. 71; Kristy, p. 102; Richard, p. 103; Corrinda, p. 107; Mike, p. 107; Geeta Soogrim-Hirsch, pp. 111 and 209; Reese, p. 166; Shantelle, p. 166; William, p. 186; Meagan, p. 197; Crystal Singh, p. 209; Tyler Hirsch, p. 209; Melanie, p. 211.

ATRIA BOOKS
A Division of Simon & Schuster, Inc.
1230 Avenue of the Americas
New York, NY 10020

First Atria Books hardcover edition October 2013

ATRIA BOOKS and colophon are trademarks of Simon & Schuster, Inc.

For information about special discounts for bulk purchases, please contact Simon & Schuster Special Sales at 1-866-506-1949 or business@simonandschuster.com.

The Simon & Schuster Speakers Bureau can bring authors to your live event. For more information or to book an event contact the Simon & Schuster Speakers Bureau at 1-866-248-3049 or visit our website at www.simonspeakers.com.

Interior design by Nancy Singer
Jacket design by Zoe Norwell
Jacket photographs by Sherwood-Triart Photography

Manufactured in the United States of America

10 9 8 7 6 5 4 3 2

ISBN 978-1-4767-2703-5
ISBN 978-1-4767-2704-2 (ebook)

For my mom, Ronnie, who hasn't stopped
encouraging, loving, and listening to me since
I was a little girl. And for giving me a strong faith
to hold on to when I was trying to make sense
of this crazy gift.

✝

For my husband, Larry, who picked up where
Mom left off. You've always made me feel so
unconditionally loved, special, and safe.
Always and forever, hon.

✝

For my kids, Larry and Victoria, for never
questioning that Mom sees dead people.
Seriously, not even a little.

✝

For God and Spirit, because without you,
there'd be no book.

Contents

THERE'S MORE TO
Life
THAN THIS

Introduction

Welcome to My Life!

If you ask me, I have two amazing abilities: I speak to dead people, and I can walk all eleven floors of Macy's Herald Square wearing really high heels. I realize the first skill is why you bought this book, so that's what I'll focus on for the next ten chapters. But before I do, there are a few important points that I want to get out of the way.

First, as I address topics related to your departed loved ones and the afterlife, know that nearly everything I understand about who we are and where we come from I owe to Spirit. This includes a lot of subjects I'd never explored before I had to write about them, but because I knew they were important to you, I offered them to Spirit. Boy, did they deliver! Another thing I did when I got stuck was to turn to a friend who helped me hone my gift. All that said, there are some specifics I either couldn't or didn't want to tackle (like when I talk about negative energy), so if I don't go deep on some topics, that's why. I also feel there's a lot about death and the afterlife that's unknown and open to interpretation. Many mediums are okay with saying their word is final, but I'm not like that. I only want to share what I think and feel, based on what Spirit has shown me and those I trust.

I realize that not everyone is going to believe what I'm about to say, but save yourself a mean email or "She's a fraud!" blog post, because I've heard it all. People say I google to get your background information. That I throw out vague situations and then work off your reactions. That my ideas about the hereafter are wishful thinking. They say I read body language and take advantage of your vulnerability while grieving. And my all-time favorite, that I'm "bothering" the dead. Let's just pause on this last one for a minute. Why hasn't it ever occurred to my critics that I'm not bothering the dead, but that they're bothering me? You think I woke up one day and thought, *Ooh! I'm going to talk to dead people for the rest of my life! That's a great career choice!?* There's more to it than you think. But I didn't write a book to prove or defend my abilities. I did this to share what I know to be true: that there's more to life than what's in the physical world.

As you'll soon find out, it took me a long time to accept my gift, but once I did, I was a pretty fast learner. I like to compare the process to putting together a jigsaw puzzle. In the beginning, it was hard for me to make sense of my abilities and fit the pieces together, but once I got started on the framework, filling in the rest of it was easy. I always had all the parts to complete the picture; I just had to learn how to make them work together. I believe that the same way some people are natural-born musicians or intellects, it's in my DNA to speak to Spirit. Would I have rather been a concert pianist or cured cancer? Of course, but what are you gonna do.

Learning to channel has come with its benefits. It's been a way for me to ease some of my chronic anxieties that were linked to

Spirit, but more than anything, it's brought countless people joy and healing, which is the most rewarding part. It's helped them believe in an afterlife, trust that their loved ones are safe and at peace, and shown them that those souls are guiding, encouraging, and loving them from the Other Side. It's given clients proof that the unexplainable things they sense and feel after a loved one dies are real, and that they're not nuts for thinking so. They even tell me they're less afraid of dying and some have a renewed faith in God. Most important, they begin to embrace life when all they knew before was grief.

None of these amazing outcomes is a coincidence, since I choose to use my abilities to deliver healing messages from souls that walk in God's white light. I believe that my intuition is a spiritual gift, because while I don't say this on my TV show, *Long Island Medium,* I accepted my abilities directly from God—who, in so many words, said that I have it for a reason. He also told me not to question them, but to trust that He would love, guide, and protect me always, so that's what I do. By the way, I believe that we are all connected to God, who is unconditional love, and it's that love which links us to our family and friends in the afterlife, because we all come from His energy. Since I was raised Catholic, I call this energy God, but if you want to call Him a Higher Power or Yahweh, go right ahead. He's a God of many names, but I feel there's only one.

Being a psychic medium doesn't always feel like a blessing, but I know it is. While the TV show has helped me put my kids through college, I've also lost friends over my abilities. What's more, I've met my share of people who want to hang out only so I can tell them what their dead grandparents are up to. And now that I'm the "Long Island Medium," forget it. Suddenly, everybody is a cousin. But I feel that we're all in this world to fulfill a purpose, and I believe that connecting people to their departed loved ones is part of my soul's journey. I'm glad I figured that out, because for a few years there, I really thought it might have been shoe shopping.

1

Me and Spirit:

A Match Made in Heaven

I wasn't born in the back of some gypsy wagon, and I didn't grow up reading fortunes on the Bayou. Listen, the only crystals on me are the Swarovski ones covering my Louboutins. I may not be your idea of a "typical" medium, but dead people don't care. They've been bugging me to deliver their messages since I was a child, and that's what I feel compelled and blessed to do.

I grew up on Long Island in a town called Hicksville, with my mom, dad, and younger brother, Michael. Mom was a bookkeeper and my dad was the public works supervisor for Nassau County. We were extremely close and still are. I was actually raised for most of my life in the house next door to the one I live in now. We have a gate in the back that connects our two yards, and Dad likes to use it so he can futz around in both our tomato gardens. When people come for readings, they sit at my dining room table, which looks out onto the back. I always say, "If you see someone out there, it's not a dead person walking around. It's just my dad!"

Growing up, I had the most loving, happy, and seemingly normal childhood. I was on a traveling soccer team and local bowling league. I loved playing with my dolls' hair—I always thought I'd be a hairdresser, go figure. I had nice friends, got good grades, and spent a lot of free time with my family. I was always with my cousins, grandparents, aunts, and uncles. On Thursdays, we'd have spaghetti and meatballs at Nanny and Pop's house; on Saturdays, I'd paint ceramics with Auntie G; and on Sundays, our whole extended family would go to Gram and Gramp's house after church to spend the afternoon eating, laughing, and telling stories.

It was like the Long Island Italian version of *Leave It to Beaver*, but with a twist that literally kept us all up at night. I used to have the most frightening dreams, which made no sense given that my days were so carefree. These were actually my first memories of seeing, feeling, and hearing Spirit, though I didn't know that's what was happening. My first vivid experience happened when I was just four years old. At the time, we lived in my dad's childhood home, which is right near the Hicksville Gregory Museum, a former 1915 courthouse that also had jail cells for prisoners in it. Some people think old buildings like prisons, with their history of pain and suffering, can hold on to Spirit. What a place for me of all people to grow up around! Anyway, I'd have a recurring dream where, from a window on the second floor of our house, I'd watch a man pace on the sidewalk out front. He'd chant my name, *Theresa Brigandi, Theresa Brigandi, Theresa Brigandi* . . . over, and over, and over again. Can you imagine how scary that was to a freaking four-year-old? I never saw the man's face, but he was always hunched over and carrying a stick with a bandanna sack on the end. He wore ragged clothes and looked like a hobo.

Spirit later told me that this dream was actually a visitation, and I now believe this "man" to be one of my spirit guides for that time in my life. This doesn't mean the spirit guide is *literally* a bum. It's more like those Bible stories where people invite in the poor, and then later find out the person's an angel. I now believe a hobo is the unassuming image that my guide took so that I'd understand the Sunday school reference and feel okay when he called my name. I was raised Roman Catholic and still practice this today, so I think my guide presented himself through my frame of reference, a little like how Spirit shows me signs and symbols during a reading now. They do it in a way that makes sense to me, so that it's easy for me to interpret the message.

When I was four, a hobo equaled a gentle, godly man—at least when I was awake. At night, seeing, hearing, and sensing one made me cry out like I was being violently attacked. Again, I don't think I was experiencing negative Spirit, and I wasn't dreaming that Spirit pushed me around or anything; the dreams themselves weren't "bad." I was terrified because I'd feel Spirit's energy, while seeing and hearing them talk to me, in this alarmingly real and personal way.

My inconsolable screams rattled my family more than what caused them, and my social life became limited. I couldn't go to slumber parties or sleep at my grandmother's house without wondering what I'd feel next. I didn't feel safe anywhere but at home, and even that wasn't a given. Besides the hobo, I also saw my great grandmother on my mom's side of the family. She'd died four years before I was born, and I didn't realize who it was until much later when I saw a picture of her. But I'll never forget her standing at the foot of my bed—she was short with dark hair and wearing a housedress. I'd scream like a crazy person when I saw her too. Poor lady was no three-headed monster, though I sure reacted like she was!

In the morning, I'd forget most of these night terrors or how long they went on. I'm told they'd pass when my mom or dad would turn on the light and rush into the room. So did this make Spirit leave? I don't know. But after a while, Mom made up a prayer to help me keep Spirit at arm's length. It went, "Dear God, please keep me safe through the night. Bless . . ."—and then I'd name all the people in our lives, and those in Heaven. And wouldn't you know, every time I said that prayer before bed, I'd sleep soundly, and so would my parents. I continued this when we eventually moved into our new home, the one my parents live in now, though I always kept the hall light on.

Even when I traveled with my family, I never got a break from Spirit. We took a lot of vacations together, including an annual camping trip with my grandparents for the entire summer. Most people at the site were lucky to have a tent with a Bunsen burner; we had this awesome trailer with a shower, kitchen, a screened-in porch so the bugs wouldn't get at our food, everything. My grandmother made scrambled eggs and French toast in the mornings, and in the afternoons, we'd have bicycle races and go tire swinging into the lake. At night, we'd play pinball at the rec hall, roast marshmallows, and sing campfire songs. I was a regular Girl Scout! But no matter how much fun we had during the day, or how relaxed I felt, my night terrors would strike like they did at home. Only this time the whole area heard me! My grandparents even warned our fellow campers in advance—if you hear someone screaming bloody murder, it doesn't mean there's a bear or maniac on the loose! It's just Theresa having a night terror. One time my parents wanted me to sleep with them in a tent, and I was deathly afraid of it. I felt safer in the camper, especially since I was seeing shadows against the canvas. I was so adamant about staying out that I kicked and screamed, and gave my father a fat lip. He was *so mad.* I was this close to knocking over the lantern and setting the whole tent on fire.

Though I handled Spirit's appearances much better during the day, they were still a surprise. For instance, I clearly remember seeing three-dimensional people walk in front of the TV. I'd be sitting on our green tweed sofa, watching *Romper Room,* when a person would pass by and then fade out. One time this happened when I had a babysitter over, and I asked her if she'd just seen what I did. She said no and gave me a funny look, so I played it off. I kind of wondered if I was seeing things or had an overly active imagination, but I didn't dwell on it. It's like when you see a shadow out of the corner of your eye, or stare at a light too long and then watch a yellow shape float across the room—you assume that you're just seeing things and don't think much of it. I also remember getting a kitchen set for Easter one year as a kid, arranging my pots a certain way when I was done playing house, and when I came back to them in the morning, they were in a completely different spot. That must've been Spirit too. Listen, I know my brother, Michael, didn't touch them!

Who's to Say What's Normal?

As I got older, I began to feel anxious and strange in my body. I couldn't put my finger on what could be causing it. I'd say to

Mom, *I don't feel right. I don't feel like I belong. I feel different.* I felt as if there was something going on that needed to be explained. One of the few places I actually felt safe and secure was in church. I even played guitar in a church folk group. God's house was the only other home, other than my own, where I felt peaceful and comfortable in my skin. I often say that if I weren't a medium, I could've been a schizophrenic or a nun. Seriously, sometimes those felt like my two most realistic options. Imagine? My parents spoiled me with so much love, but that didn't take away from the fact that I sensed something about me was off.

Sometimes I'd ask God, *Why is this happening? Why do I feel so afraid all the time?* But I'd never get mad or angry at Him, or lose my beliefs. That wasn't how I was raised. I don't like to use the word "religious," but I did come from a strong faith family. I was taught to say prayers at night and before every meal. My parents also had an open mind about all spirituality. It's funny, because not all Catholics do. But to us, faith, spirituality . . . it all comes from God.

When I wasn't at church, my anxiety could get so bad that I didn't want to leave the house. I didn't know when I'd sense or feel something, at any given moment of the day. I realized that every place I went came with a different sensation, and I sometimes felt like I was being watched. When I'd tell this to Mom, she'd sit me down and say, "Your safe place is *you*." I could go anywhere, because I was my grounding force. For a long time, that mind-set worked.

Even still, I was clearly seeing and sensing things that other people weren't. When I was out with my friends at the mall or the bowling alley, I'd ask if they saw a man walk by or heard some-one call their name, because I secretly had, and they'd go, "Uh, no.

What are you *talking* about?" Or sometimes I'd receive a message, which I'd assume was just my own random thought and not realize that it had any meaning, or that I'd even thought of anything, until it was validated later. For example, if I was on my way to the fair, I might hear a voice tell me, "Don't eat the cotton candy." I'd ignore it, and then a friend would tell me the cotton candy made her sick. But even then, I just assumed that I got better hunches about people and situations than maybe some friends or strangers did.

Again, I believed that I was my safe place. So seeing, hearing, and sensing something around me all the time became my normal. Doctors have always said that our bodies are built to adapt; if a feeling or experience goes on for long enough, the brain learns to disregard it, work around it, or just treat it as normal. I know now that seeing and sensing Spirit isn't most people's typical experience, but it was routine for me, and I didn't have too many people disputing it. As a child, my family and friends just laughed when I'd occasionally say strange things, but never pursued the subject much further. (Mom recently joked that my abilities give a whole new meaning to when I used to say there was a monster, imaginary friend, or ghost in my room!) And for as many times as friends didn't agree with what I'd heard or seen, I did have family who had similar experiences because they're also sensitive. In fact, my cousin Johnny Boy used to jokingly call me and my cousin Lisa "freaks," and nicknamed us "Para" and "Noid," when we told him we'd see or feel things. We also used to go shopping separately and come home with the same outfits! But at the time, all Lisa and I knew was that we had unusual, shared experiences that made encounters with what we now know is Spirit just part of our lives. As for my smart-aleck cousin Johnny, he was living in my grandmother's house ten years later and saw her standing in the hall when he was coming out of the shower. Who's laughing now?

When my peers became mouthy teenagers, things began to change. Between the ages of about twelve and fourteen, I began to feel less comfortable with what was happening around me, mostly because of how people reacted to my observations. My family was still blasé about stuff I said, but when I'd casually ask if a friend saw or felt something, they'd be like, "No, that's weird, there's nobody there. Nobody hears or sees things the way you do!" What once seemed normal now wasn't, so I decided to block my experiences out altogether. I didn't say a special prayer to make Spirit stop or anything; I just didn't acknowledge Spirit's attempts to communicate with me. Keep in mind, this was before every TV channel had a ghost-hunting show and John Edward was a household name. People didn't talk about this stuff. Nobody, including me, could've guessed what was really going on. It was never part of a comfortable, mainstream conversation.

By the time I was sixteen years old, I was lucky that I hadn't lost a lot of loved ones, but this also means that I didn't have recognizable Spirit visiting me. When Nanny, my father's mom, died, I was devastated. We were very close, and everyone missed her a lot. After she passed, my dad's older sister, whom we call Auntie, had a psychic come to Nanny's house. I didn't know why at the time, but I now think it was to get in touch with her. I didn't want to go, and I felt a little afraid—mostly because I didn't know what a psychic really was or did. But I knew I'd feel safe at Nanny's house, so I went anyway. And for the first time in a long time I didn't block Spirit.

I felt Nanny's energy and soul near the window, and my family kept asking me why I was by the drapes when everyone else was at the kitchen table. They also asked me whom I was talking to, though I don't remember what I was saying. (It's similar to how I can't recall most of what Spirit says after I channel for others.) After a minute of this, my family had to interrupt me in their usual, teasing way. They kept it lighthearted and didn't freak out.

"Theresa, who are you talking to?"

"I'm talking to Nanny."

"Sure you are. Nanny's dead."

"I *know* she's dead, but I'm talking to her."

Auntie and my cousins might have been confused but didn't make it a big deal. I was known to blurt out crazy things, but was this any stranger than having a psychic over for coffee? They were clearly open to spiritual conversations that I hadn't considered yet.

When I think about this memory now, I can physically smell Nanny's house and see everything in it—the plastic-covered furniture, marble end tables, her sparkly dining room chandelier, a painting of *The Last Supper*, and those gold drapes. It was very gaudy Italian. And as I tell this story, I get a vision, like a quick filmstrip, of Nanny standing at the stove, smoking her cigarette all the way down to a really long ash that's dangling over a bubbling spaghetti pot. She'd let that cigarette burn until only the filter was left, and yet the ashes never fell into her gravy. She loved her jewelry, and in my memory, she's wearing all these diamonds. Like me, you know?

After my little encounter with Nanny, I went back to completely ignoring Spirit. My uncle Julie died during my senior year of high school, and around that time, my anxieties began to get much worse than they'd been. I developed random phobias, many of which had to do with feeling claustrophobic. The night terrors had long past, but I still had restless sleep habits. Instead of waking up screaming, I'd jump out of bed, feeling like I couldn't breathe to save my life.

Then Along Came Larry

My eighteenth year wasn't a total disaster, though. That's when I met my husband, Larry! When Auntie had the psychic over that first time I saw Nanny's soul, he told me I was going to meet someone much older than me with a beard and mustache. Back then, I thought the psychic was being a wacko, since I was dating someone at the time and didn't even like facial hair. But two years later, I met Larry, and you better believe he had a beard, mustache, and was eleven years older.

It was love at first sight. Larry had this awesome hair that was tight on the sides, fluffy on top, and long in the back. He was also a sharp dresser and had a nice body. He looked like a clean-cut biker! He says I was a cute little sparkplug who made jokes and lit up a room. Larry worked for his family's business, an oil company, and I worked part-time in the customer service department. I never went to college because I was too afraid to leave my family and comfort zone. I dreamed of becoming a hairdresser or legal secretary, but that meant commuting into Manhattan for the good jobs, which was way too overwhelming for me—trains, elevators, skyscrapers, traffic jams . . . that was not my world.

Larry tells me he used to look forward to coming to work to see what I was wearing, because I was in my Madonna stage. I used to wear skintight pants, big belts, a fishnet top that draped off my shoulder, and fingerless gloves. Like in that movie *Desperately Seeking Susan*! But just because I was distracted by love doesn't mean my anxiety went away. I tried hard to suppress it, but that only made things worse. I didn't want Larry to think I was crazy, and I was still occasionally wondering if I was. Sometimes I saw figures or heard things, but at this point I was in such denial that I was fully convinced my mind was playing tricks on me.

I decided to see a therapist, who, session after session, basically said there was nothing wrong with me. I'd tell him, "Ben, there *is* something wrong with me. I don't feel right." He'd ask me all about my childhood, and I'd explain that it was idyllic. My friends and family now? Great. Dating? Fun and exciting. Work? Fine! The best cause we could find for my chronic unease was that I came from an anxious family, so maybe this kind of thing was genetic. But the guy couldn't give me one good medical or psychological reason why I felt as severely bad as I did.

I couldn't keep my anxiety attacks and laundry list of phobias from Larry for too long, especially when we were in the car or other enclosed spaces. I seemed to feel my worst when my mind was at rest. If we were on the Long Island Expressway during a traffic jam, I'd get a frown-y look on my face knowing that I was about to freak out. Then I'd scream bloody murder, and even if the car was moving, I'd beg and plead with Larry to pull over so I could get out right away. I even did this on double dates with other couples in the car! My anxiety was not shy. The panic attacks would eventually pass, and it helped that Larry always kept his cool. He didn't know what was causing me so much stress, the same way I didn't, but I'm just glad he didn't get spooked and leave.

Larry and I got married when I was twenty-two. Right away,

I'd startle him in the middle of the night. I'd wake up yelling, jump out of bed, and run around the room yelling his name and crying for help. Then the moment would pass, and I'd come back to bed and forget it by morning. I talked in my sleep too. I never let Larry pull the covers over our heads, not even as a joke. Once he threw a blanket over us when we were watching TV, and I began screaming. He never did *that* again. But hey, Larry knew anxiety came with the package, and he loved me just the way I was.

In Sickness and in Health

My husband says that although I made us take the hospital stairs instead of the elevator when I was in labor with our son, Larry Jr., I was unusually calm and in control during childbirth. I was twenty-three when our first child was born. My anxiety went up and down after, but I generally felt better, now that I had the new responsibility of taking care of a child. I could even travel okay.

Ever since I was a junior in high school, I was always ashing a cigarette with my manicured fingertips. I never drank or did any type of narcotic, but smoking was my vice. I stopped when I found out I was pregnant with our son, but two or three years later, I went back to smoking when those familiar stress levels snuck back. I thought smoking cigarettes would relax me, even though it seemed to make my chest feel heavier, which only increased my anxiety.

I stopped smoking again when I got pregnant with Victoria, had her at twenty-seven, and went back. My anxieties became horrific. The worst they'd ever been. I can remember a horrifying incident at Disneyworld when I hadn't traveled in a while. We got to our hotel room with the kids, and I immediately started freaking out.

My mom and aunt had to take the train from New York to meet us and calm me down. As if having a severe panic attack weren't bad enough, I also took it out on my husband. He says I needed a scapegoat. The kids had never seen me that bad and looked terrified to watch their mom unravel in front of their eyes.

In December 1999, I became deathly ill for no reason. Now, I am not a sick person, I don't do sick. Even when the kids were young and brought home nasty germs from school, I rarely caught their colds or flu. But this was the weirdest thing. I was getting ready for a wedding one morning and I was fine; then suddenly out of nowhere, I had a 104-degree temperature. My dad literally carried me to the doctor's office. I was on my back for two weeks, which was hard since my son, Larry, was nine and Victoria was five. My husband was a big help as usual, but it's not like I had the luxury of staying in bed. I don't even remember the first delirious week of all this. And during the second, I just lay there. I couldn't walk, eat, or go to the bathroom. I also couldn't smoke.

In hindsight, I believe God was detoxing my body during this time. Drugs, smoking, narcotics—all that stuff funks up your aura and mucks up your energy. And smoking, specifically, turns your aura gray. I stayed away from cigarettes when I got better. This doesn't mean I was a joy to live with. I remember Mom saying to me, "You're such a bitch without nicotine. Go back to smoking!" You know what I said back? "God's making me stop!"

That rationale came flying out of my mouth. I checked myself. *Where did that come from? Why would I even say that?* That's when I knew quitting was an act of God, because those words didn't come from my brain. And with that, I haven't touched a cigarette in thirteen years.

When I channel Spirit, I do it from a place of the highest good, and that requires my body, mind, and soul to be healthy and pure. Looking back, I wouldn't have been able to develop my abilities if I continued to fuel my body with anything negative, like cigarettes. But at the time, all I knew was that God wanted me to stop smoking. Certain foods began to make me ill too. Doritos and Wendy's made me feel dizzy and light-headed, like I couldn't focus. I hallucinated when I ate MSG. When I was pregnant with our son, Larry and I were walking out of a Chinese restaurant and had one of those surreal conversations that reminded me of when I was a kid.

"Hey, did you see that dog in the car?"

"What dog?"

"Don't you hear him barking?"

"Hon, there's no dog."

"It's a husky. He just winked at me!"

I later learned that Siberian huskies are considered to be very spiritual dogs, since they're so closely related to the wolf, which Native American tradition says is the highest spiritual teacher in the animal kingdom. I suspect the MSG helped trigger my vision because it's a chemical, and when people alter their chemistry, it can do some crazy stuff to their soul.

A Serendipitous Encounter

At twenty-eight, I was a hot mess. I'd just stopped smoking and my anxieties were nonstop. I didn't want to leave the house and was in a constant panic that something bad would happen if I did. My therapist called this "anticipatory anxiety," which is when you anticipate future events in a way that causes you to feel anxious, and that interferes with your ability to function in everyday life. The thought of going to work, the butcher, or a birthday party made my mind reel.

One night, Mom had a candle party—like a Tupperware thing, but with scented candles—and I decided to go at the last minute. She lived next door, so *this* I could do. Mom's friend Pat Longo is a spiritual healer and works with people who have physical or emotional ailments, including chronic anxiety; she also teaches classes about living a balanced, positive, and fulfilled life that includes meditation and healing. Like me, Pat also decided at the eleventh hour to go to Mom's event. All these last-minute decisions don't say much for her parties, do they!

I told Pat about my anxieties and how sick I'd been, and though I'd known her for years—her son and my brother grew up together—she had no clue about the anxiety I suffered as a child, and certainly nothing about how I sensed Spirit. She put her hands over my head and began to channel healing energy from God. For three weeks after, I felt so calm that I wanted to do it again. But when I called to make an appointment, Pat told me I didn't need another healing, that there was nothing for her to mend within me. She asked if I wanted to take her spiritual awareness class instead to give me some perspective and balance in my life. She suspected Spirit communication was causing my distress, but didn't tell me that right away.

Whatever Pat did to me made me feel better, so I decided to go for a class—why not? I also trusted her with my well-being because my family had known hers for years. If Pat were some random spiritual healer, I wouldn't have been able to believe in her or her evaluation of me. I put on a good face for friends and family, but I was still fragile on the inside and wouldn't have felt safe with just anyone. I also knew I'd feel secure in Pat's classes because my mom had taken her course a few years before. She was actually one of Pat's first students, though she only went to learn more about feeling positive and healthy from the inside out. My dad and us kids used to rib her, like, "Oooh. You're going to your voodoo class tonight." Pat says Mom was starting to touch the surface of her own abilities by the end, but she put her spiritual energy into working with the church instead of developing them any further on her own.

After that first night in Pat's class, I got sidetracked and didn't go back for, um, a year. When I finally did, the classes were held on Wednesdays, and every week there would be a downpour. One of my phobias was driving in the rain, so I cut class for that whole first month. But in my heart, I wanted to make this work, so I practiced driving in thunderstorms, up and down the block. I was ready to go back to Pat's the next month, though it continued to rain every Wednesday.

I think Spirit made it rain to help me break through my fear, on my way to honing my gift. This shouldn't surprise me; it always rains during milestone events! There was a monsoon during my son's baby shower and my daughter's Communion, and Hurricane Hugo hit on my wedding day. It wiped out St. Thomas Island, and my honeymoon was canceled. Even when I taped *The Tonight Show* a few years ago, which was intimidating and such a big deal for me, it poured cats and dogs. Leno's producers assured me that it never rains that much in LA in October, and wouldn't you know, the minute I was done shooting at five p.m., the sun came out.

I'm a What?!?

"You're a medium," Pat told me during class one night. A lot of people were discovering their own gifts, and this was mine. "You have the ability to speak to dead people. If you can learn to control the energy around you, you can learn to control and understand your anxiety better."

This was the first time I'd ever considered that my anxiety and all that stuff I saw when I was a kid, and forced myself to ignore, could be related. Who knew there were real, physical consequences to blocking what I'd been seeing, hearing, and sensing?

Pat explained that one reason ignoring Spirit gave me anxiety is that I channel Spirit through my chakras. Ideally, it enters through the crown, or head, chakra, flows through my entire body, and then releases through my words. But when Spirit was trying to deliver a message, it would channel through my crown, and I'd block it in my chest, which would cause my heart to race or give me those crazy palpitations. My chest would also feel heavy and compressed, as if an elephant were napping on it. I don't even know much about all the chakras, just that I need to keep the crown chakra, third eye, throat chakra, heart chakra, solar plexus chakra, spleen chakra, and root chakra aligned and balanced so I don't freak out.

Pat also said the *type* of channeling I do was causing me to have panic attacks. There are lots of ways that mediums experience Spirit. A "clairvoyant," for instance, mostly sees visions, and a "clairaudient" primarily uses her hearing sense. Pat explained that I'm "empathic," which means I *feel* Spirit most, and use my other senses to fill in the blanks. For instance, a message might begin with me feeling very restricted in the throat area, which means there is a soul that would like to tell me that they passed via a death connected to the throat, that they were unable to communicate prior to their passing, or they did not get to say good-bye (one symbol for me can mean a lot of things—more on that later). But if I felt my throat close without knowing that this was Spirit's way of delivering a message, all I'd know is that I felt like I was choking, which triggered a panic attack.

So I'd be having a normal conversation with someone at the grocery store, say, and all of a sudden I'd feel like I couldn't breathe or that I was being strangled. I now know that's Spirit trying to communicate with me, but fifteen years ago, I was just like, *I have to get out of here!* As I said earlier, this could happen even when I was asleep. As soon as I removed myself from the situation or woke up, I was good, but it was a quick fix. I also thought some places felt better than others because I had random anxieties, but it was really the energy changing in each spot, often based on Spirit's presence. As for the phobias, I think they're usually about associations, quiet moments, or past lives. I may have either felt Spirit in that exact place, or a similar one, which is why anticipating it made me nervous. My Catskills camping memory contributed to my tent phobia, and riding in cars or being silent in an elevator forces me to sit still without distractions, which is when I'm most open to Spirit. During a past-life regression, I also learned I was a prisoner on a ship during a torrential storm, which explains why I'm afraid of rain. I could go on, but I'll spare you all my phobias and explanations! Suffice it to say, all these situations made me feel out of control, and so all of these things caused me to panic.

As for my anxious family members? I suspect they're also sensitive, since I believe my gift is genetic. They're also very faith-based people, which increases your awareness of Spirit.

I continued to attend Pat's courses every Wednesday, as Larry watched the kids. I felt calm at her house, since I knew that if anything scary happened, Pat could make me feel better. In class, I began to give people messages from loved ones, and right away, channeling made me feel normal. But I was afraid to try it anywhere else. I still needed Pat as my safety net.

Physically and emotionally, I began to slowly heal. My anxieties became less dramatic. Larry saw a difference in me, and I told him channeling Spirit seemed to be a big part of the answer. He was like, "That's cool, hon. If you think talking to dead people makes you feel better, keep doing it." Larry was also raised Catholic, so I'm not sure he believed in Spirit, and was more likely appeasing me, but he was supportive, which is what ultimately mattered.

Six days a week when I wasn't in class, I had to cope on my own. Since I hadn't fully accepted my gift yet, I was still prone to the occasional meltdown. I remember when my first cousin Lance got married, we planned to go but at the last minute, I could not get in the car. The kids were dressed, and Larry had mapped out the fastest route. But I didn't want to drive that far, and my whole family was so upset. I paced for hours. Finally Larry said that if at any point I didn't want to continue, we could turn around and come home. I reluctantly agreed to go.

Cell phones were still new at the time, and I insisted on taking one in the car in case I needed to call Pat to talk me off a ledge. I remember hearing Faith Hill's new song "Breathe" and thinking, *That's exactly what I need to do, just breathe.* I made Larry play it over and over. I now think it was Spirit telling me to relax already.

When we pulled into the hotel parking lot, my whole family was waiting out front. I remember seeing Gram, who was alive at the time, standing at the window waving at me. I can still see the smile on her face, as if it were yesterday. She died a few years ago, but whenever I get over anxiety-related hurdles—like taking a tour bus across the country or sitting in a tent in my backyard—Spirit makes me remember Gram standing at that window, beaming with pride.

Give Spirit an Inch . . .

To help control the energy around me, Pat taught me that I had to set some boundaries with Spirit that I still use today. I can't dictate which guides, angels, or dead people talk to me, or what they want to say, but I can control whether I acknowledge them and how I do that. So in the beginning, I said to Spirit, *I'm going to set aside a time every day at four o'clock for you to communicate with me. I'm going to light my white candle to protect everything in God's light. I ask only for the highest good of all concerned. And I only want to channel souls that walk in God's white light.* And you know what? For the most part, Spirit respected that, so I became more comfortable channeling too. We were developing a real give-and-take relationship.

Whatever I sensed while I was meditating, I wrote down on a pad of paper. Pat taught me how to do automatic writings, which is when you basically take dictation from Spirit. Channeling through the pen is an easy way to speak with Spirit, especially when you aren't fully comfortable with "hearing" messages in your mind and can't always tell the difference between your thoughts and Spirit's. You'll see me do automatic writing during readings on TV with my little notepad, since it helps me focus; when I channel, I'll scribble down words that Spirit wants me to use to make a point.

Another major thing I asked Spirit to do was stop presenting itself to me as three-dimensional people—an image like you or me. When I first started reading others, I'd be brushing my teeth, look up, and suddenly see a man standing behind me in the mirror. That was so startling! So I told my guides that if I was supposed to embrace this gift, they'd have to find other ways to show me things. From then on, I saw Spirit as figures in shadow instead. I don't mean negative "shadow people," or the scary dark masses that whisked away the bad guys' souls in *Ghost*. The images I see are like silhouettes, or like a chalk outline at a crime scene but filled in with a cloudy shadow you can see through. Its energy feels very positive. In fact, because I only want to serve the highest good, I don't see negative Spirit and try to avoid them at all costs. I don't like Halloween parties or historic haunted houses, and you couldn't pay me enough to touch a Ouija board. In the same vein, I'm always asking that things be protected in God's white light, so I never even get negative information during readings. Only good things, that's all I want.

I began to develop a "vocabulary" with Spirit to understand the signs and sensations they were sending me. I took on more of Pat's clients and began sharing the unbelievable, moving, and often hilarious stories with Larry. He asked lots of questions, and I could tell he was becoming more invested in what I was doing. Frankly, we were both amazed I could speak to these souls in the first place! In a lot of ways, I was on a clear spiritual path, but we were growing in it together.

Holy Sheet! I Really Am a Medium!

Though I only liked giving readings in class, one day I let it happen in real life. I was in Bed Bath & Beyond, and I remember feeling like I couldn't take a breath. I'd established with Spirit that this is a sign that someone's passed from the chest—heart, lungs, breasts, a filling up of fluid, or a drowning even. At one time, I would've gone into a tailspin—abandoned my cart in the middle of the aisle, hightailed it out of the store, sped through stop signs crying, and beat myself up for the whole drama once I got home. But that day in BB&B, I told myself I'd be okay. I thought about what my mom used to say: *Your safe place is you.* And then I heard a man's voice.

"Tell my wife I like the ones on the left," he said.

Nobody was there.

Just then, an older woman came up to me with two sets of sheets. She told me she'd just lost her husband after forty years of marriage and was redoing the bedroom. She couldn't decide which sheets he'd have liked better. I suggested the ones on the left, and it made her so happy.

I didn't tell the woman that her husband told me what to say. I like my baby steps, if you can't tell! But at that moment, I knew Spirit would continue to place people in my path who needed to hear messages from their loved ones, like this woman. I also believe my own Spirit guides were giving me my first real test, and I passed! The best bonus of all? My chest felt normal after delivering the message. I channeled, released the energy, and went on with my day.

After taking Pat's classes for five years, and reading her students, it was time to share my ability with others. I felt confident that what I was doing came from a higher power. There were also signs that made me feel I was being guided by the divine. I was thirty-three years old when I accepted my gift, and Jesus was thirty-three when he died. I live off Jerusalem Avenue. Pat suggested I make business cards and get a separate phone line for my venture. The last four digits of this number were 6444, which I thought was perfect because I was born in the month of June (6), and I believe 444 is a sign of the angels. But the day my phone was set to be turned on, the guy told me he had to change it. I was so bummed, until I realized that the last four digits were the sign of the cross. It's worth mentioning that one reason it took me so long to accept my gift was that I struggled with why I was chosen to have it in the first place. I kept thinking, *Who am I? I'm no one special. Why was I chosen to do this? Why is this my journey?* And being raised Catholic, you don't contact the dead. So I think Spirit was also sending me "religious" signs to assure me that what I was doing was okay and, in many ways, guided.

From the moment I began seeing clients in my home, my family was laid back about it. If people asked my kids what their parents did for a living, they'd say, "Dad owns a business importing Italian foods, and Mom speaks to dead people." So natural, like I was a teacher or something. Larry also overheard some readings at the house and began coming with me to my small venues. After that, he said it was hard *not* to believe in what I did. He'd get especially impressed when Spirit had me talk about health or human anatomy, because I didn't go to college. I also don't read books, since reading relaxes my brain and clears my mind in a way that lets Spirit communicate with me, and then I can't focus on my book! So where would I learn this stuff, if it didn't come from Spirit?

Being a medium also helped validate a lot of "unusual" experiences for my husband. Larry saw his grandmother's soul when he was ten years old, but was never sure it was real. He shared a room with his brother, and she was standing at the foot of his bed. Larry thought it was his imagination, and actually forgot about it until I accepted my gift. He's also learned a lot about déjà vu. When Larry was young, he'd be in places he hadn't been before, though he had clear memories of them and couldn't explain why. Now, if he feels anything "strange"—like déjà vu, gut instinct, chills, good timing, coincidences, or even a hand on his leg or tug on his shirt, he knows it's Spirit. In 2001, Larry was diagnosed with a brain tumor and not only did he survive, he overcame most of the nerve damage that it caused. He credits more than his doctors for his recovery.

My favorite change in Larry, though, is that my tough, tattooed, motorcycle man has become more emotionally sensitive to *everything* for some reason. *The Color Purple* makes him cry and don't get him started on how much he loves our family. The guy's a sap.

The Start of Something Good

Though I've finally embraced my gift, I'm far from perfect. I have fewer panic attacks, and I'm much more independent. But I still don't like elevators or enclosed spaces, and I'm deathly afraid of the dark (no pun intended). I sleep with a nightlight and TV on, and I keep all the doors open except the closet. I also don't go into a deep sleep at night. I toss, I turn, I hear things, I feel things. And if I dream, I don't remember it. Larry says when my alarm goes off at six a.m., I get right up—no stretching, no snoozing. It's as if I'm happy that I don't have to be in that bed a minute longer. I try to be the best Theresa Caputo I can be, but there are plenty of days I come up short. I'm a medium, not a saint!

As someone who doesn't exactly hide her big personality, I've found it fun and interesting to channel souls that have distinct characters and stories. I love meeting new people, and being a medium can make me feel like the hostess at a really important gathering. Children's souls, especially, have told me, "My parents have been to mediums, but I like channeling through you because you let my parents see *me*." People can feel their loved ones and how they acted or spoke when they were at their best. I'm not saying this is because I'm better than other mediums—no no no no no. I feel that all mediums channel and connect with Spirit differently; one isn't more skilled or better than another.

I realize that I have a lot to be grateful for. I'm glad that I can share this gift with other people, though my family likes to joke that I don't give them much of a choice when I stop them in the gym, dentist, or at the mall! I'm glad that Spirit continues to keep me on my toes, and with every single reading, they teach me something new. I also feel thankful that I have such an easygoing personality, or else it might be harder for me to accept my unusual abilities. As a rule, I don't question or overanalyze anything—I let life be simple. If you handed me a bottle of hair spray and asked how it worked, I'd say, "Listen, I don't care how. Does it work? Yes? Great." I don't need to know how, when, why. It is what it is, and that's it. I treat Spirit communication the same way.

But, enough about me. Let's get down to Spirit!

Don't Shoot the Messenger

So how do I communicate with Spirit, including your loved ones? People ask me this all the time, and it can be hard to put into words since channeling is an ability that comes naturally to me. It's like how my daughter, Victoria, is a competitive gymnast. She can do high-flying dismounts, crazy back handsprings, and flip through the air. Yeah, she practices twenty-five hours a week and does a bunch of exercises to help her improve on her raw talent, but she started with an innate skill that made her un-freaking-believable at swinging and tumbling. And if you ask *her* how she does it, she'll say, "I don't know. I can just do it." Her gift is part of her. It works the same for me, talking to dead people.

Before I get into specifics about what it's like for me and my clients when I channel, I'd like to explain how the process works. During a private or group reading, Spirit—mostly your loved ones who have died, but also my guides and other divine souls on the Other Side—makes me sense, see, hear, feel, and know things in ways that most people don't, so that I can deliver their messages to you. Usually more than one soul channels in a session, and I have no control over who steps forward. I might talk a mile a minute, but the reading isn't about me. It's about what Spirit wants *you* to know. I'm just the physical body that a soul uses to let its voice be heard. I ask only that Spirit communicate with personality, for the highest good of all concerned, and that they tell me the messages that will bring you the most peace at that moment in your life.

My job, then, is to explain what Spirit shows and tells me. Souls do this through my frame of reference, which means that all of the messages I get are filtered through my personal experiences (I always say that when I channel, everyone sounds Italian and Catholic!). If I've never heard a term, phrase, name, or come across the kind of situation that Spirit's describing to me, it may take a minute for me to communicate the message in a way that you can connect with and then interpret. If I'm describing something to my clients that they don't understand, I ask them to tell me. It doesn't make me right and them wrong, or them right and me wrong. Spirit is never wrong, first of all, in what they try to communicate to you. What could be incorrect is how I've "translated" the signs or feelings they use to get their points across. When a detail seems fuzzy or unclear, I'm the first to say, "I don't know what this is about, but here's what they're showing me!" If we're still drawing a blank, Spirit has me come at the topic another way. I leave it to you to make sense of the overarching messages, though, because only you know how they fit into your life. I might suggest a few meanings, but I'm never the last word on any of them.

The wild thing is, Spirit always gets its point across. If we don't understand a message at first, I don't worry. You may connect the dots later in the session or when you get home. I know Spirit makes me say every word I do for a reason. Here's a good example. One time a woman came to me whose father died very suddenly. He wanted me to tell her, "Don't feel that if I were diagnosed any sooner that I'd be alive." I felt as if he'd passed from a skin disease, but he showed me that he died after hitting his head. He also kept saying, "Theresa, can you believe this is how I died?" I didn't know what the guy was talking about, because I intuitively felt like he didn't die from hitting his head and yet that's what I was being shown. *Madone,* can you imagine how confusing this message seemed? But it wasn't my job to interpret it—just deliver the words. Turns out, the woman's dad hit his head getting into his car, which gave him a cut that refused to heal. When he went to the doctor, he learned that the cut wasn't healing because he had stage-four melanoma (it's one of that cancer's identifying symptoms). He died two weeks later.

Hey, Spirit, What's Your Sign?

I've met enough skeptics in my life to know that not everyone buys what I do, so I want to try to give you a sense of what it's like for me when I communicate with one or more souls. I'm not here to make you believe in mediums, though my guess is that if you bought this book, you're at least a little curious! I don't mean to be rude, but I don't really care if you believe in what I do. I'm just here to share what I feel to be true.

Before I start channeling, I begin with a short speech for a few reasons. For one, I do this to explain how I receive messages and how you can interpret them. My monologue is also my sign to

Spirit that I am ready to work. I use this ritual whether I'm reading for one person or a venue of three thousand. At this point, your deceased loved ones start to clear out my own personal thoughts, feelings, and emotions, and they begin to replace them with signs and symbols of things I have experienced here in the physical world so that I can relay their messages to you.

Throughout a session, Spirit uses a vocabulary of signs and symbols to either (1) validate their relationship to you, and/or (2) deliver a specific message to you. I call this collection of signs and symbols my "Spirit library." These signs can come with certain feelings, since I'm empathic, as I've explained, but I'll get into that part later. I translate my signs as best as I can, and then deliver the message to you. Again, it's your job to interpret how the meaning is significant. It's a little like piecing together a puzzle or solving a Scooby-Doo mystery. Wait, does that make me Daphne?

When Spirit's validating their presence or relationship to you, I ask them to be clear, unique, and specific. I don't let Spirit give me obvious validations; if they do, I ignore the clue and ask them to try again, with more precision. At this time, they might mention something you said in the car on the way over or a specific piece of jewelry that's special to you. For example, one time a grandmother's energy came through and showed me four-leaf clovers in reference to her granddaughter, who just happened to have the woman's Claddagh ring in her pocket. Or once Spirit told me a client had something pinned inside her bra, and the woman said she pins an evil eye and horn into her bra every day! She said she never leaves home without them, since she believes the evil eye keeps people's negativity from reaching her, and the horn guards her from others' bad wishes and boomerangs it back to them. Holy moly! I freaked myself out on that one.

The only thing I find frustrating is when skeptics use the validation process not to demonstrate that Spirit's around us when we need them, but that I'm a real medium. They might ask a loved one to have me mention the name of a movie or an object they've hidden nearby, and I rarely entertain these games. I understand where they're coming from—you think I don't find this ability to be a little wacky?—but I always say that even if you don't get what I do, please respect it and withhold negative opinions or decisions about me until you've experienced Spirit with an open mind and heart.

Now, some signs from my library are cut-and-dry, like Sonny Bono, who's my symbol for a person passing in a ski accident, since that's how Sonny died. And then there are signs that have multiple meanings. Roses, for example, are my symbol of love and devotion, but the rose's color can have different meanings. So, a red rose for me is a symbol of an anniversary, either someone's wedding or of a passing. Yellow is my symbol for someone's name—be it Rose, Roseanne, Rose Marie, or a name with the word "Rose" in it. If I see yellow roses and feel like they're connected to someone special, you're about to hear from, say, a grandmother named Rose *or* Spirit could be acknowledging that they knew you had yellow roses delivered to the house from someone special. A lot of times when Spirit mentions a recent event, it's the soul's way of saying that it was with you at the exact moment you had that experience. All of this may sound a little complicated, but it's harder to explain than it is for me to experience, which is really all that matters, right? The amazing thing is, when you're sitting across from me, it's unbelievable how fast you catch on!

I created my vocabulary by assigning meanings to certain words and phrases, and then through trial and error, Spirit helped me add new ones. The more explanations I can assign to a symbol, the faster we can speak with your loved ones and the more messages I can deliver. Let's use horses as an example. Whenever Spirit used to show me a horse, it usually meant that someone liked horses, was an equestrian, or bet the horses. But one day, I went through all the meanings with a client, and when he didn't connect with any of them, Spirit showed me the strangest thing— an outline of New Jersey. So just like that, horses also began to symbolize the Garden State. Why? Beats me, but if it works for Spirit, it works for me. I went through the same process with oatmeal. It was always a symbol that meant someone liked to eat the gloppy cereal—obvious enough. But then once when I said that in a session, the client said no, so Spirit then made me feel like I was pacing up and down a driveway every day. I asked the woman if the deceased was very regimented, and when she said yes, Spirit established that oatmeal would now mean that the person really liked oatmeal and/or that the person liked a routine. Seems random to us, but listen, maybe Spirit thinks it takes a lot of discipline to eat a bowl of Quaker Oats!

This doesn't mean that every new symbol that Spirit shows me makes it into my library. Sometimes images are just part of a message that you need to interpret. For instance, I was buying a new iPhone, and the district sales manager happened to be at the store. I picked up that the man's father and father-in-law had died, since two father figures stepped forward for him. I knew one soul was his father's, but the second could've been an uncle, a grandfather, an older friend. . . . So I tell the guy, "There's a father figure with your dad, and I just saw the other straighten your tie." I suggested that this could mean Spirit was calling him a spiffy dresser, but he quickly corrected me. He said his father-in-law actually *collected* ties, and he used to always tie the son-in-law's ties for him. Stop it! Mystery solved, but here's the thing. This story is also a good example of why I try not to interpret things for people on my own. Even though Spirit gives me hints, I can't possibly know what something as arbitrary as a tie would mean to you.

While interpreting some signs takes guesswork, other times a cigar is just a cigar. I once asked a woman if she was pregnant with a son, because Spirit showed me a blue blanket, which is my sign for having a boy. Turns out, she was pregnant with a *girl,* but her husband had just put their son's *blue blanket* in the dryer before I arrived and said this to validate a soul's presence. I find that numbers are also reliably clear symbols. They connect with special dates like birthdays and anniversaries of those who've passed and are still in the physical world. They can also be an age. For example, if I see the number six, it could mean June, the sixth of a month, a six-year-old's birthday . . . you get the point.

Look Who's Talking

Not only do I use signs and symbols to communicate your message, but at the same time, Spirit "speaks" to me through a sixth sense—a kind of feeling and knowing. When I get information, it feels like incredibly strong intuition, but I never doubt or overthink it. I trust that Spirit has me say things for a reason. I simply feel and know what Spirit wants to communicate, and then I open my mouth and let it spill out. Sometimes I'll make a connection or deliver a message when I'm not even trying. I had a client tell me her mom knew how to light up a room, and when I offhandedly said, "The belle of the ball!" the woman told me her mom's name was Bella. I don't know how my brain works, but I don't think other people's do this—at least not as often.

There are many ways that I use my sense of feeling and knowing. When dead people talk to me, often to identify themselves, they first make me feel the emotional bond that you shared with them in the physical world. I might feel "a mother energy" in the room, which could be a mom, grandmother, mother-in-law, or even an aunt who was *like* a mother to you. Spirit can also make me feel a situation that's affected you somehow. If their message is about surprising news, they can make me feel the shock that you experienced during that interaction. I can physically feel how a person died too. If my throat feels restricted, it could mean someone passed from an issue related to the esophagus, choking, a hanging, or that he couldn't express himself at the end of his life. If my mind goes blank, it means the person had Alzheimer's or dementia, and if I feel pressure in the head, then someone died from an aneurysm or brain tumor. Sharp pains also point to different conditions. If I feel one in my side, it's either related to a kidney or lower back issue; the pelvic area links to liver or bladder problems; and if my legs go numb, it means someone had leg swelling, or was paralyzed or an amputee. After one of my bigger shows where I channel a lot of souls, I feel like I've been poked and prodded all night.

Because Spirit's energy is on a different, higher, and faster energy frequency than ours, Spirit's words and thoughts come to me very quickly. They can also send me a lot of thoughts, feelings, and symbols at once. This tends to happen when Spirit uses a term, name, or idea I've never heard before, so I have a lot of clues to choose from when delivering a message. I don't get word-for-word sentences, and I don't have common phrases or platitudes assigned to feelings or symbols. Spirit can also speak to me at the same time that I'm asking them for clarification and talking to you. My response *is* the question—an intuitive reaction that doesn't require words to be understood. This is because Spirit doesn't talk to me from a mouth like ours, even if I see a full body apparition; ideas pass from Spirit's soul to mine. They communicate using their thoughts and emotions, simultaneously, and we can understand each other without using language the way you and I do. For this reason, dead people from other countries can talk to me in Chinese or Russian, and I understand them perfectly, as if I have a degree in foreign languages. Once in a while Spirit whispers in my ear, but I don't know why they bother. Nobody hears them but me!

When I'm filling in the details of Spirit's message, a soul may speak to me by engaging one or more of my other senses. I might smell gardenias though there aren't any in the room, or watch a series of events like a filmstrip or flip book, so I can describe how an event unfolded. Sometimes a soul overcomes all my senses so I can see, hear, feel, smell, and taste things at once. If Spirit makes me feel as if I'm holding a baby in my arms, I can feel and see the blanket and smell the newborn. This is my "symbol" for when a soul held an infant at the time of its passing or right after the baby died. Spirit may also put me into a situation in my mind's eye, while using multiple senses in ways that still surprise me. One time I did a house clearing, and a female soul didn't want me to enter the home. I sensed that she was standoffish and wanted me to stay outside until she decided it was okay for me to enter. Then I literally felt the soul grab my arm, and the homeowner said this happens to her too. Next, Spirit placed me in a bed, in my mind, and I instinctively knew the soul inappropriately touched the woman while she was sleeping. I asked her if this kinky piece of information was true, and she said it was. I'd never heard that one before!

During a session, Spirit might talk through me with their speech and mannerisms. Without realizing it, I might make a face that someone's brother used to make or do a quirky, recognizable dance that a person did while he or she was still in the physical world. During a live performance in Atlantic City, I walked right past a man, turned to him, and said, "Oh, hi, *mamala!*" The guy was floored. After the show at the meet and greet, he pulled me aside and said, "I haven't heard that term in thirty years. My mom used to say that to me." I have no idea what made me say this, to him no less, or what *"mamala"* even means. But it was important that he hear it, because that was his mom's soul speaking through me. She'd passed thirty years prior.

When I deliver Spirit's messages, I have no filter—zero, zip, none. I picture my cranium like spaghetti in a colander. My brain's the pasta, the water is the information pouring over and through it, and then the messages come right out of the holes that are my voice, expressions, and mannerisms. I should learn to watch my mouth, though. A lot of times there's no proper way to say the stuff Spirit tells me, so I just blurt it out. I was doing a restaurant venue of eighty people, and there was a girl there who lost her brother. I turned to her and said, "Your brother wants you to get rid of your boyfriend. He's no good." But get this—the boyfriend was sitting right next to her! So I announced that if I had four slashed tires at the end of the group, we'd all know who did it. The girl broke up with the guy four months later, but that's beside the point. Or is it?

Believe me, I'm well aware that the information I'm spewing

can be fast, emotional, surprising, choppy, confusing, and piecing it all together can feel overwhelming. You may also doubt it at the time or not recognize how it fits into your life. That's why I tape all of my sessions, so that you can go over the messages at your own pace. A man once left the funniest voice mail on my answering machine: "I came to you four years ago for a reading, and you were talking about a bunch of shit that made no sense to me at the time, but it's all happening now!" Everything Spirit says is for a reason; it may just take a few days or years for you to realize it.

Once a reading is over, I remember few specifics about it, or else my mind would be full of stories about other people's dead loved ones, and that's no way to live. In fact, as I retell stories for this book, I'm not using my "memory," so to speak. Spirit mentally puts me back into the setting, using all my senses, so that I can retell the stories with as much detail as possible.

I Spy with My Little Eyes . . .

During a reading, I can also physically see Spirit. To me, they appear as see-through shadows with hard edges, as I explained earlier. So I might see the silhouette of a woman's head, with her flipped hair, but no definitive features like eyes or a nose—unless Spirit wants to communicate something about the person's eyes or nose, either to validate its presence or send a message about it. I also really like watching Spirit interact with a living person. I might see a soul lean forward and kiss a friend on the head, or sit in a mother's lap. It's such a tender expression of an ongoing relationship and bond, and of the soul's ability to communicate with warmth and character too.

Sometimes Spirit will tell me what they look like on the Other Side. This happens a lot with children who've passed. Like, Spirit might show me that the soul has a smile that's missing a tooth or has braces, which usually tells me how old the child would be in the physical world. Does this mean the soul literally has braces in Heaven or lost a tooth over there? I'm not sure. What I do know is that the way Spirit portrays itself to me is either how we remember them or how the soul *wants* to be remembered. Souls might also show themselves like this to talk about a specific moment, or bring comfort to the listener. Maybe the child's sister lost a tooth or got braces, and Spirit wants her to know that it's aware of that special milestone.

Souls are radiant figures of light on the Other Side, which may be why they sometimes appear to me as a round ball of energy coming out of a wall, before they morph into a shadow shape. But they always want me to describe them in a way that their loved ones will fondly remember them. Time is measured differently in Heaven, yet Spirit often shows me how much a soul has "grown" since it left our world. This also comes up a lot with a kid's soul. I don't believe the soul is physically growing or chronologically aging the way we do here, because our souls don't have bodies in Heaven. I do get the impression that the soul is spiritually growing and advancing as a result of the lessons it's learned here and on the Other Side. Young and growing souls who've passed also show me that they're not sick anymore. A lot of times they'll have me reference a picture where they look happy and healthy, and they'll say that's how they want to be remembered. They might show themselves to me as being dressed in a specific outfit to validate that it's them, but I don't know if they're literally wearing these clothes on the Other Side just to hang out. Then again, some hypnotists who can regress people into past lives have said that souls may wear their favorite outfits for the fun of it!

What's in a Message?

People come to see me for their own reasons, but they all seem to leave with more insight than they expected. Some need closure, while others want to know how a person died if it's still unresolved. The majority come to find out if their loved ones are at peace. There are also way too many people who want to find out if their spouses are cheating. Look, if you're seeing a medium for a second opinion on this, I bet you don't need me or your dead mother to tell you what's up. My hope is that you at least walk away knowing that your loved ones are still with you, that they're willing to communicate, and that life goes on in Spirit after your physical death.

Though some people come to a reading expecting to hear from a certain person or receive a specific message, the takeaway can be completely different because Spirit tells you what you *need* to hear at the time, not what you *want* to hear. I did a reading once at a large venue, and I kept hearing the words "Bruno" and "hockey." I asked if anyone connected with this. A man close by raised his hand and said that his name was Bruno and that he coached hockey. Perfect. He also said he'd just lost one of his players. I sensed that he was devastated, and that the boy's death could keep him from doing what he loved. I asked if he wanted to give up coaching, and Bruno told me that after the child's death, he really did. The boy's soul made me tell him, "You can't give up. Those kids love you and you treat them like your own." A person may not know what he'll benefit from until a reading is over, but I promise you this: it can be life changing.

During a first reading, I've found that Spirit likes to lay a little groundwork and heal old wounds. They might talk about the spouse you married after the person died, stuff going on in family members' lives, or maybe details about your job. They'll also talk about how they're at peace if this is a reason you're seeing a medium. They'll basically catch up, make sure you're okay, and let you know that they are too. If you find the session comforting or need reassurance or support at another time, you can come back for a second reading six months to a year later to talk about things that have happened since you last connected. For me, I won't channel any sooner than that, since I feel we need to give Spirit time for their souls to spiritually mature on the Other Side, which helps them communicate with us better. You also need time to heal and process what you learned from the experience. During a reading I did at a restaurant, I channeled a man's mother; it brought him so much comfort that he made an appointment to see me privately. The man hadn't spoken to his sister in five years, and when I channeled his mom, she let him know that she knew about their friction. The man saw me again, the next year, for another session and shared that after our last one, he was able to rekindle a relationship with his sister. Now he comes once a year just to connect with his mom. He loves knowing that she's not missing out on anything in his life, including the good rapport with his sibling.

No matter when a client comes to see me, Spirit always brings up topics, conversations, and questions that figure prominently in your life. It's their way of telling you that they know what's going

on, and that they're always with you, supporting you, and inter-
ceding for you. They're aware of what you've been crying, laughing, stressing, and thinking about—but unless there's an urgent
message related to these topics, Spirit can feel that it's enough to
simply recognize the issue when I channel them. During a private
reading once, Spirit showed me my symbol for somebody altering
a piece of jewelry and told me that it might be changing hands. I
asked the woman if she'd redesigned an heirloom to give away, and
she said that she'd considered redoing an old bracelet to give to
her daughter when she got married. In this case, Spirit was simply
acknowledging that they knew about the gift. That's it. The soul
wasn't giving its opinion on the setting or whether the present was
a generous idea. Some people project their own thoughts, feelings,
hesitations, and fears onto Spirit's messages, and it can distort the
meaning. If your dead grandmother wants you to know that she
doesn't like your new necklace, remembrance tattoo, or newly renovated house, believe me, she will say that.

A lot of people also take what Spirit says as gospel, and you
can't hang on every word they're telling me, because again, their
messages are based on an interpretation of the information that
I'm feeling and being shown. Spirit may nudge you in a direction, but more often than not, they want to help guide you toward
making your own choices and decisions—not make them for you.
You do have free will, and interpreting Spirit's messages as literal
advice instead of gentle direction and support can lead to confusion and frustration. I did a reading for a woman at my house, and
from the moment she sat down, I could feel her anger. I tried to
ignore it, yet the first thing Spirit had me say was, "Your mom says
your husband isn't going anywhere." I thought this would be good

news! Not exactly. The woman looked like she wanted to lunge across the table and rip my eyes out. Apparently she'd gone to a world-renowned medium a few years earlier, and she was told that her husband was very sick and no longer meant for the physical world. The medium was right that the man was ill, but the woman was also in an unhappy marriage, and ultimately, she decided to stay with him because of the medium's prognosis and what she thought was advice. Cut to twelve years later, and the woman never got her divorce and here I was, telling her that the man she didn't love was here to stay! When she shared her story with me, I told her that things might have unfolded differently for her husband's health, his relationship with his kids, or even her own sense of obligation or guilt had she chosen to leave. But the bigger lesson here is that you shouldn't lunge into a huge decision based on what someone else says—dead or alive.

Souls also tend to bring up topics you're struggling with to encourage you to do something that will bring you a sense of calm. Again, this is a form of gentle guidance, not an urging to do one thing or another. It's like the time I felt a sharp pain in my breast and heard the word "recheck." Spirit told me nothing was wrong with my client's health, but I did feel she or someone she loved was due for a mammogram. The woman told her mom about the reading, and her mom admitted that she'd been secretly experiencing breast pain for weeks after a mammogram, was nervous about it, and kept putting off a second visit to the doctor. Spirit's message prompted the woman to see her MD, and her "recheck" results were fine. But this was Spirit's way of getting a message to the mom that she should see the doctor, if just for peace of mind, and that they were with her during the visit.

I only ask for good things in my readings, so I've established that the only way Spirit can bring up something negative, like an argument or a bad thing that will happen, is if they are giving us information about the situation that will help us make it better. I once did a group reading at a woman's house, and Spirit told me that her husband was going to change jobs and go in a completely different direction—but not to worry because he'd be much happier in this new position. The woman laughed at me and said Spirit didn't know what they were talking about, because her husband was top brass at his company and made a very good living. Well, two weeks later, she called to tell me his company downsized and he was let go. The good news was that he found a job right away that gave him much more time to spend at home, and it had been a real blessing for the family. He also felt more fulfilled in this position than in the one he left.

I've learned that Spirit doesn't want us to have regrets. When we die, our souls in Heaven can finally look at the big picture of their life in the physical world and see it for what it was—how everything happened for the greater purpose of helping others and learning certain lessons that would help us evolve into more enlightened souls. Maybe Spirit's desire for us to live without heavy remorse is why souls always show me other possible outcomes of a bad situation. This happens when a client second-guesses decisions they've made for themselves or loved ones, or wonder how life might have played out "if only." The most poignant example I have of this is a story I like sharing about one of the first souls I channeled outside of Pat's class, a seven-year-old boy named Brian Murphy. If he were still with us, he'd be the same age as my Victoria.

About eleven years ago, Pat came with me to meet Brian's wonderful parents, Bill and Regina. Months prior to his passing, Brian began saying strange things. First, he repeatedly told them that he wanted his wake to be held at a certain funeral home they passed on their way to the town swimming pool. Brian was healthy, but no matter how often and fervently his parents said the boy's death was a long way off, he persisted.

Naturally, they found this odd. Then, as the Murphys prepared for their summer vacation, Brian asked his parents to buy him a suit. He wasn't receiving Communion for a year, and there were no formal holidays in their future. Now the Murphys were scared. So when their family vacation rolled around, on the heels of such uneasy talk, you can imagine how hesitant Bill and Regina were to go; it sounded as if their precious seven-year-old were preparing for his own funeral. But the family never thought in a million years that their worst fears would become a reality. It was on that vacation that Brian drowned in a lake, in front of hundreds of witnesses.

When I met the Murphys, they were making themselves sick over what might have happened to Brian had they skipped that trip. But when I channeled Brian, he did the most amazing thing—he explained how he might have died if he didn't drown. One scenario was that he would have been kidnapped and found in the trunk of a car, which was a specific, recurring nightmare of his mom's. He then had me explain that he could have died in a car accident with his dad on the way to baseball practice, which would have made Bill obsessively wonder what he could have done to prevent the crash. Brian explained all these scenarios to make sure his parents understood that no matter how he died, this was the "best" one for his family's grief process. Just as important, Brian said it was his destiny to die young, and it couldn't have been prevented.

One message that comes up time and again from souls is that there is nothing you could have done to prevent their death and that they want you to embrace life without the burden of fear or guilt. Brian helped lighten his parents' load by doing this. On the Other Side, there are few mistakes—just choices that have colored your journey here. I think this is another reason Spirit doesn't tell us how to live our lives when I channel; they know we need to make our own decisions so that we can determine the course of our fate.

Spirited Personality

I always make sure Spirit communicates with laughter, attitude, and the traits they were known for in the physical world. You spend enough time crying and being sad over the loss of your loved ones. I wish I could give you back the family and friends that you've lost, but obviously that's not in my skill set as a medium. So the only thing I can do when I channel is make you feel like you're with them, feel their souls, feel their senses of humor, and I take that part of what I do very seriously. I want to make the piece of your soul that feels like it was ripped out, stomped on, and put back in your body recognize that your friends and family are "themselves" on the Other Side. And if they passed from an illness, showing the disposition they had before they got sick also tells me they're at peace. If they were in a bad place, they'd say negative things. At least that's how I see it.

The fact that Spirit keeps their personalities in Heaven is a big reason why no two readings are alike; each soul's character is so unique! I'll get a ballsy soul that comes on strong, she doesn't beat around the bush—and sure enough, her family will say that she was pushy in the physical world. Or if someone was shy or unexpressive, that soul will pull a hat over its eyes, not finish sentences, or feel like it's pulling back from me.

One of my favorite examples of how souls retain their personality quirks and charms happened when I did a group reading for a bunch of sisters and their mom after their father had died. His soul came through and said that when Mom goes on her cruise, he'll be with her. He described how amazing it would be—the whole family would be on a large boat, and because it was a Disney cruise, Mickey Mouse and Cinderella would be there too. The woman was very confused, since she hadn't planned a vacation for herself recently, much less such an indulgent one. "I don't know what my husband's talking about," she said. "I can't afford to go on a trip like that." But her husband's soul kept at it. He was insistent! After lots of sideways glances, the kids burst out laughing. "Okay, Dad, we'll tell her!" they said. The girls had planned a surprise birthday cruise for the family for their mom's seventieth birthday. "This is so typical," the mom said. "He could never keep anything to himself!" Clearly, he's still into blowing secrets from the Other Side.

Another time, the souls of a husband and wife came through to validate their presence to their daughter with a very specific shtick. The dad had me yell, "Bingo!" at which point Mom's soul said, "They don't have bingo on TV. It's *The Price Is Right*!" The daughter laughed so hard and said that game show was her parents' favorite. She used to call them when they were alive, and they'd say, "We need to call you back. The Big Deal is on right now!" When the daughter's son was born, he came into the world right before the Big Deal aired, and the family joked that the baby was the Big Deal of the day. The mom's soul also had me add that she likes Bob Barker better than Drew Carey as a host. Hey, that certainly wasn't me talking! I think they're both great.

And though there's a lot to be happy about in Heaven, people who were crabby or bossy here don't seem to become unusually chipper. I'll never forget when I channeled a woman's parents, and I got a grumpy vibe from them. I asked the daughter, "Were your parents cranky?" And at the same time that the woman said, "No, my parents were *wonderful*," her husband mouthed, "Hell yeah, they were cranky!" Grief can cause us to romanticize the deceased, so I took the husband's word on this one. In a three-thousand-person venue, Spirit also had me point directly to one guy and say, "You, your father wants you to get up. Is that your mom? He wants her up too. He says you're a frigging idiot for what you did to the lawn." Turns out the man had just bought a new ride-on tractor and destroyed an acre of his land because he didn't know how to work it. Then he told his wife to stop knocking on her son's door and bothering him so much. Though Dad was doing his thing in Heaven, he still thought of himself as the man of the house.

I really love when Spirit tells animated tales that make everyone giggle, especially since I like to keep messages lighthearted. During a group reading, Spirit once had me say, "What's with the pinky ring?"—and the room erupted with laughter. The family had just been gossiping about how their cousin swiped her dead brother's ring and hocked it. The man had given it to the brother while he was alive, but now that he had passed, the sister took it and sold it. The brother knew about it on the Other Side, and though he wasn't upset or hurt, he wasn't going to let the family think it slid past him! Can you believe it? At the end of the day, no matter who's died, you're left to live the rest of your time here without that person, and it's hard. I think Spirit figures there's no better way to heal than for them to talk to us with the personalities they had when they were healthy.

The More Spirit, the Merrier!

When I read for a group, whether it's in a room of ten or four thousand, a lot of Spirit want to talk, so I'll usually go with the ones that bug me the most or ask Spirit to use a technique that I call "piggybacking." This is when multiple souls want to relay the same message, so they'll band together to get it across to many people. Here's how it works. Let's say we've identified a person's father who's coming through, but as you're hearing the message from him across the room or even down the same row, you're thinking, *Gee, that sounds just like my dead cousin Nikki*. If this happens, I ask that you accept that the message is from the first person's father *and* your cousin. Piggybacking doesn't just console a lot of people at once, though. It's practical. In a reading, I want to deliver as many messages as I can and move the energy through the room at a good pace. Who wants to waste time repeating the same thing to different people?

Spirits that piggyback may not have been connected here in the physical world, but because they are connected to you, they're connected on the Other Side when preparing for a group reading. I don't believe a message has to be from just one soul, especially since they've shown me that they work really well as a cluster.

Spirit can also come forward, recede, and play off each other's energy. They channel together like old pros. In my largest venue readings, it's amazing how organized your family's souls have been! I also believe Spirit will help orchestrate who comes to the readings and sometimes where they sit. You can't miss how certain types of deaths—which is how I initially validate your loved ones to you—are seated together, which makes piggybacking easier. In one section of a theater, there will be multiple women who've lost children, families whose loved ones had Alzheimer's, or even friends who've died from similar freak accidents like a falling object. It sounds wild, because it is. And Spirit's behind all of it.

What I love most about group readings is that you get to hear so many incredible, compelling messages that you can't help but feel touched by all of it. I also find that Spirit is a little more fun during group readings, especially during the private, smaller groups. In a room of ten to fifteen people, I can channel anywhere between twenty to forty souls in a two-hour period. But there are so many different, lively, and dynamic personalities around that souls with stronger energy can help those with less to communicate better by letting them use their energy. Sometimes I have souls that channel for an entire hour, and nobody else comes through; other times, a soul might stay for a short time, go away, and then come back and talk a mile a minute! It's like the soul recharged its batteries.

When a reading is over, I can hardly remember what I've said, seen, or felt for too long after, because again, they're not my feelings, thoughts, or emotions. Unless the message is part of a really mind-blowing or emotionally gripping session, whatever information Spirit sends me isn't something that's stuck in my head forever. Know too that you take your dead friends and family with you when you leave a session, show, or my house. For some reason, it's always the husbands who remind me to take all the Spirits with me, and I'm always like, "Listen, pal, they're not *my* Spirits. They're your dead relatives. They're staying with you. I got my own problems."

But for as long as I've done this, there are still times I'm blown away when souls drop in for a visit. I'll never forget when, during a group reading, I saw a man sitting at the end of the dining room table. He wanted me to tell the host that he knew she was concerned about her best friend's husband. Then he looked at me and said, "I'm going to be with my father now." I told this story to the group in real time, and the host, overwhelmed with emotion, excused herself and left the room upset. When she came back, she said that just forty minutes before the session began, her best friend called to say that her husband died and his last words in private were, "I'm going to be with my father now." Are you kidding me with this? If that's a parlor trick, I'm one hell of a magician.

Who Are the Spirits on
the Other Side?

When I accepted my gift from God, I told Him that I only wanted to know things about Spirit and the afterlife that could help people heal from a loved one's death. That's it, and that became my mission. I don't need to know every detail about how this works— how many guardian angels you have, if Jesus hangs out with Buddha, if your in-laws still bug you in Heaven. Talking to dead people can be overwhelming enough for me as it is. Unless God insists, and He hasn't yet, I don't want to stress myself out with more. I'm also not the type of person who likes to overanalyze most things in life, whether we're talking about the Other Side or what my son is up to when I'm not home. I realize things aren't always black-and-white, but I also feel that we need to leave room for faith.

To me, my gift is about aiding and enlightening others as best as I can. It's similar to when people go through a powerful experience like cancer, poverty, or infertility, and make it their life purpose to raise awareness and support for those in the same situation. They don't need to become experts, teachers, or doctors to change lives. In a similar way, I've had a lot of crazy experiences with Spirit, so I hope to "raise awareness and support others" with the info I've gathered, to help and inspire them on their journeys.

I mention all this because I realize that not everyone thinks the way I do, especially when it comes to wanting to know who's with your loved ones on the Other Side. Does the Blessed Mother play bridge with your dead grandpa? Is your childhood shih tzu at their feet? I know the answers to some of these questions when I'm asked, but if I don't, I tell people the truth: I'll find out when I get there. I also turn to Pat for answers, since she's a healer, teacher, and dear friend. I consider Pat my mother of Spirit, since she helped me hone my abilities and taught me a lot of what I know. I trusted her with my health and soul when I was at my lowest point, and I still turn to her for support today. So at points in this chapter when I need to fill in gaps, I've tag-teamed with her. Between the two of us, we'll do our best to give you some insight on this topic.

People who've had near-death experiences, plus past-life hypnotherapists who've gathered info about what we do after we die, say that Heaven is full of many souls with many purposes. No surprise there, since Spirit's told me that Heaven is a much vaster place than we could ever imagine. But I will only touch on Spirit that Pat and I have personally experienced in one way or another. That means there are probably many other entities, with many other duties, that I won't talk about in this section. But angels, guides, religious figures, your loved ones, God—those, I'll cover. All of these beings are Spirit.

As you learn about Spirit, you'll notice that some of their duties seem to overlap, though they all watch over and direct you throughout your lives in some way. I imagine that the structure in Heaven is a little like a well-run company, or society even, that's organized with many tasks and positions—some souls oversee, some strategize, some train, others collaborate, some are worker bees—and their collective skills and responsibilities accomplish big and important goals. But these rules and roles aren't always set in stone. As with any successful organization, there's room for those in power to change the way things run, if the moment calls for it.

Although I'm a practicing Catholic, I don't want to make this about religion. I can't emphasize that enough—and in fact, this is God's preference, not mine. But you have to realize that while I've experienced a lot of what could be considered "biblical" Spirit, I believe I'm exposed to these entities because they're related to the life I or my clients lead. Remember, Spirit speaks to me through my own experiences. If I were a Buddhist or Hindu medium, I wonder if Spirit might present itself differently or if I might have different teachers. Also, I tend to channel a lot for Catholics, simply because there are so many in the United States that they happen to contact me more than people of other faiths, so Spirit shows me their religious symbols more than those of others. Some spiritual beings, however, like angels, guides, and God, cut across nearly all faiths.

What Happens When We Die?

Before I get into a Heavenly roll call, I want to quickly explain some of what I'm told happens when we die. I don't know too much detail on this, but I will briefly share what Spirit's said, since it will help the rest of this chapter make more sense! Later in the book, I'll get into topics like God, Heaven, life lessons, and the circle of life more deeply.

When we die, our souls peacefully detach from our bodies. We're greeted by the familiar souls of family and friends who died before us, and then glide toward a brilliant, eternal light that is God. On earth, we are a piece of God's energy, but in Heaven, our souls are one with His. In the physical world, I'm told that we have a primary guide—some people call it a "master guide"— who's helped us throughout our life; he or she is also there to greet us when we get to the Other Side.

With our primary guide, our soul reviews and evaluates the journey we had in the physical world, and we get to see how our various actions affected others. We experience what we made others feel—pain, happiness, confusion, understanding—and how it's related to what our objective was in that lifetime. Our soul's ultimate purpose is to learn lessons that spiritually develop our soul over many incarnations in the physical world—lessons about patience, joy, faithfulness, selflessness, and so on. Part of our purpose is also to help others learn lessons, make good for things we've done wrong, and grow our soul in a way that aligns with God's. We prepare for this by reviewing a basic outline of what our life will be like—one created by God and reviewed with our primary guide. We've also chosen the bodies and families that help us accomplish our goals.

When it's time to learn new lessons, Spirit tells me that we'll again have the choice to either learn these in Heaven or reincarnate and come back to earth in a new body, with new experiences.

If we choose to come back, we'll learn our lessons faster than we would in Heaven. In every life, we have free will and we'll encounter various crossroads that let us make choices, related to our lessons, that can take us down one path or another, with the same destiny and overarching lessons in mind. During it all, our guides, angels, and loved ones protect, guide, deliver messages, and intervene. They show us, and elbow us into, situations that encourage us to make different choices that move us ahead and affect our future decisions. Eventually we die, and then it starts all over again.

The Greatest Love of All: God

God gets his own chapter—hello, he *is* God!—but I want to mention Him here, first. He goes by many names to many people—God, Yahweh, Creator, Allah, The Source—but no matter what your religious beliefs are, Spirit says there is only one true God. From what I can tell, it doesn't matter what religion we are, as long as we choose a faith rooted in Him.

When we go to the Other Side, we're instantly at peace because we're with and part of Him. God is unconditional love, and every thought, feeling, and experience you have in Heaven revolves around this powerful premise. It takes a very long time for our souls to grow toward God, and that development is closely guided by the souls and angels on the Other Side.

Once during church, the priest said in a homily, "I've never seen the Holy Spirit. But I'm telling you about it, because I know it exists"—and that clicked with me. It was really validating, because I feel God's presence in a similar way. I don't hear or see Him, but I feel Him in the core of my being and have connected with Him on a level that feels really different from when I channel guides, angels, saints, or your loved ones. I can tell that His energy comes from a higher dimension. And I always know it's Him, the way my priest knows the Holy Spirit, and my dad knows a good tomato.

The times I've spoken to God, the most I've seen with my eyes is a white light with golden edges that fills the room. And I just feel different—it's hard for me to explain. I feel a tremendous amount of peace that's almost paralyzing in a good way, and then I feel a big, God-like presence. Then that sense of knowing I talked about kicks in, and I just know it's Him. My demeanor and tone change too. If this happens during a session, I become very serious, and I'm usually not! I take what I do very, very seriously, but my readings are always lighthearted and fun. My voice is usually playful, but when I speak from God, it becomes more careful, precise, and to the point. Listen, I don't want to be the one who misinterprets what He has to say!

I get the chills thinking about the few times I've felt God's presence during a reading, especially when a person is struggling with his or her faith. During any session, Spirit gives people information to help them grow, but when those words come from God, they're particularly special. I'll never forget the mother and daughter who came to see me, because their son/brother was killed by a drunk driver, just as he was pulling into his own driveway. What are the odds? The man had worked overtime too, so they felt that he shouldn't have even been at that place, at that time—though as Spirit tells me, our destiny is generally set. As I read them, I felt the most unbelievable, peaceful sensation coming from a different dimension than I typically channel from. I knew it came from a higher power, and it felt so good that I almost wanted to go there!

Just then, the son's soul said, "God is coming. He wants you to give a message to my mother." I delivered His words: "You can be angry with Me all you want, but your son is with Me. He's safe and at peace. I also want you to continue doing My work. People need you." The daughter began to sob and said that on their way to my house, she and her mom talked about how the mom had lost faith in God. Prior to her son's death, she'd volunteered at church and given so much back to her parish, helping so many along the way. But after the tragedy, she became very angry with God and stopped going to church. God gave her permission to be upset with Him, but He also wanted her to reconsider her faith and good works.

Above and Beyond: Angels

Angels are active and involved in our lives on a regular basis and in amazing ways. They "work" directly for God as messengers, protectors, rescuers, and interceders. There are many types of angels, though none have ever lived on earth the way our guides have (more on them later). They're Spirit, not physical beings, so they don't have bodies like we do. I'm told they can take on the appearance of animals or people.

There's an order, or ranking, to the population of angels that includes archangels, guardian angels, cherubim, seraphim, basic angels, and others (that's not the ranking, that's just a list of angels). I know there are high-ranking angels, or archangels, who have various jobs and missions, and they are above other angels that inspire and intercede for us as well. Pat has regular experiences with Archangels Michael, Gabriel, and Raphael. Michael, for example, is a protector and adept at performing acts of justice and power. She calls on him for assistance when she has difficult clients or people with something very dark attached to them, like when she worked with a young woman who played with a Ouija board. Pat also tells clients who are fearful to call on Michael when they're nervous or anxious about something. Gabriel is connected to kindness. Raphael is in charge of healing, so Pat calls on him for her clients since she's a healer.

Spirit tells me that angels are powerful and seriously busy. They offer protection, guidance, deliver messages, encourage us, strengthen us, and help to answer our prayers. I hear so many stories from clients who've survived the unthinkable—car accidents, for example, where they walked away fine but their vehicle was wrapped around a tree. Was it an angel who protected them? A loved one? It depends, and I think it can be both. Spirit's told me that this kind of intervention is orchestrated by angels and guides who may send a loved one to intervene, if they don't do it themselves. My friend's son, for instance, was in a very bad car accident with her brother-in-law when he was six years old. After the crash, when he was stuck in the car, he said he saw his great-grandmother standing outside. "Mommy, your grandma protected me in the accident," he told my friend, though he'd never met her. I feel an angel sent her. But angels aren't just around us when we need them; they're with us all the time. I've also never seen angels use wings to fly to a person's rescue, or for any other reason; this doesn't mean that it can't happen, I've just never witnessed it myself. I've only seen angels drift through a space as energy, like clouds moving across the sky. Archangels, however, have shown themselves with wings.

I'm told there are also guardian angels assigned to every soul and they are with you throughout your many lifetimes. Even though I'm told that guides have walked in this world and angels haven't, I've often wondered if guardian angels and guides are the same thing, since not all angels have wings and guardian angels sound like a religious interpretation of the same role that guides play in generally spiritual beliefs. I'm not too sure, to be honest. What I do know is that they love being acknowledged as part of your life. Guardian angels are always trying to help you out and guide you on your spiritual path with great love. They also provide protection by prompting your intuition, creating coincidences, and intervening in your world in times of need or danger.

I have an angel that guides me named Solerna who was specifically assigned to me. When I see her, she shows herself to look like the angel on my business card. I'm told that she's an Angel of Sunshine and Guidance. She brings me peace when I need it and always encourages me to show my playful side. When I communicate with her, my mind's eye fills with a bright, white light with a blue aura, almost like a cloud that's backlit in a movie. It's different from the God light because His is rimmed in gold, beams more brightly, and it makes me feel that I'm surrounded by love. Solerna reassures me that everything I do and say is guided and protected by God, since I believe angels are sent from Him to carry out tasks and deliver important messages.

For this reason, I think of Solerna as a direct liaison between me and God. I consider her an immediate pipeline if a friend is sick or if I need urgent help, but I also ask her for daily guidance, along with my other guides, especially when I channel. Solerna has come to me with messages, like when she told me that Gram was going to die. On Sunday, June 7, 2009, Solerna told me Gram would die on my birthday, which is June 10. My grandmother was ill at the time but hanging on, so I actually thought I misunderstood the message; I thought that Solerna may have meant that *Pat's* mom was going to pass, since she was also sick and seemed to be getting worse. On the next day, the eighth, I wasn't able to see Gram but called, and her voice was so strong when she told me she loved me. She also kept acting as if it were my birthday—Gram was very worried that she hadn't gotten me a card—but it wasn't. She'd confused the days. Gram died the next day, the ninth, which is the day before my birthday and the same day her brother Anthony died. We buried her on St. Anthony's day, June 13. The point is, Gram never would have died on my birthday, but like Solerna said, I believe she was supposed to die on that Monday, the day she *thought* was my birthday, but waited until the next one.

Divine Intervention: Souls of Faith

It's no surprise to me that figures from religious or holy texts, or what I call souls of faith, come through for me during clients' sessions. Some are more evolved souls than others, based on the lessons they've learned and roles they've played in this world and Heaven.

From what I'm told, the most evolved Spirit has made great sacrifices on earth, completed their spiritual journey, and then ascended to the highest levels of Heaven. They help masses in this world and include figures like Jesus, Buddha, Muhammad, Mother Teresa, and the Virgin Mary. Once in a while, these souls step forward when I'm channeling, and even stand next to them. The

Blessed Mother, for example, comes through a lot for me. I see her dressed in blue and white, or she shows me my sign for her—shiny, white rosary beads. She appears mostly to those who pray to her, or whose deceased loved ones did. She shows up for validation and to assure people that even if their prayers haven't been answered, they've been heard. A lot of times she'll step forward to say that she came for a soul and guided it to God. If a parent is comforted by the Blessed Mother, she often greets their child when they cross over.

Pat's own mother had an experience with the Blessed Mother, when Pat took her to a healer in Long Island, at a time when she was suffering from inoperable breast and bone cancer that had metastasized throughout her body (Pat wasn't aware of her gift at the time and, in fact, this was the first time she experienced a healer). Pat's mom says she didn't remember much about the healing and thinks she fell asleep, but when they got into the car to leave, the healer ran out and said, "Do you pray to the Blessed Mother?" Her mom told her yes, every day, and the healer said the Blessed Mother was in the room with them, but she felt so overwhelmed by her presence that she didn't say anything. After that, Pat's mom lived fifteen more years without any pain; her oncologists were stunned at the miraculous recovery. And even during Pat's own healings, she said clients claim to see and feel souls of faith like the Blessed Mother and St. Padre Pio, an Italian priest who experienced the stigmata and was said to have heavenly visions and gifts (archangels, guides, and others have been seen too). It doesn't happen all the time, just when it's needed most.

I also have a different connection with Jesus, a very highly ascended soul, than I do with other souls. There've been times where I'm certain that God is present and He then delivers specific messages—

that it's okay to be upset, that a person needs to begin to heal, that it's best to pray with gratitude, whatever it may be. But with Jesus, he's just . . . around. His presence is always in the room. If the mind's eye could have peripheral vision, I'd say I could sense him both teaching and watching me from afar, almost off in a corner. I also see Jesus as a teacher because of my faith, but if I were a medium who practiced another faith, I think that I might sense those ascended souls in the room instead.

Some of the most well-known saints also come through for me, either looking like themselves or often as a symbol I've assigned to them, for validation or to deliver a message that's related to what they're best known for. Like with the Blessed Mother, saints come through if a loved one or the person I'm sitting with prayed to that saint, and/or if either one has statues or medallions in connection with that saint. A black habit with a red rose is St. Thérèse, also know as "The Little Flower." When I see a man in a brown cloak, that's my symbol for Moses or a strong, biblical male figure like an apostle; it's also what I see just before other male saints begin stepping forward. I channel St. Jude, St. Joseph, St. Michael, and St. Christopher a lot too. They mostly present themselves if someone has a connection to them—maybe a woman put a scapula of St. Michael around her father's neck as he died, or prayed to St. Jude when her husband was sick. Like the Blessed Mother, saints also like to step forward to talk about prayers being answered and heard.

On Your Side: Guides

Guides have a similar job to angels, except angels are closer to God. Guides tend to get their hands dirtier on a regular basis, closely guarding your soul and directing you on your path in the physical world. They keep you on track with your lessons and give you reassurance, help, and protection throughout your day and in a very hands-on way. They arrange opportunities for us and make us aware of them. They place people in our paths and help us make the right choices; they're not allowed to interfere, just gently guide.

Intuition, gut instinct, coincidence, hunches, a random or fleeting feeling—those can come from guides. It comes across as an internal voice that suggests you call one doctor over another, or as the impulse that makes you take a different route to the mall and then you later learn that you avoided an accident by doing this. Now, God also gave you free will, so you can opt not to listen to these signals and do your own thing instead. But you want to live the most fulfilled life you can while you're here, and I feel that trusting your guides is a sure way to avoid feeling stuck, acting judgmental, or becoming a generally miserable or unkind person. They'd never urge you to live this way.

Unlike angels, most guides have lived in the physical world. They can appear as any age, and come from any culture, era, or geographical location. I don't think our souls have an assigned sex until they enter our bodies (though we may feel more comfortable with one gender over another), so our guides can appear as a man, woman, or animal, as Native Americans believe. Spirit also tells me that a guide can be a loved one reassigned to you or that passed before you were born. There are psychics whose main gift is to channel guides, and they say that if a person loves and feels close to angels and other religious figures, then they, Jesus, the Blessed Mother, or other highly ascended religious figures can act as guides too.

Though there may be more, Spirit's told me about two types

of guides—primary guides, or what some call "master guides," and then other Spirit guides. Everyone has this first type of main guide who's with you from when your soul enters your body until the end of your life in the physical world. These guides teach and manage you in a way that supports your soul. Primary guides also choose an identity that will best accomplish what you're here to do, or that you can most relate to. They aren't judgmental, but like any good teacher, they will motivate you and understand where you're coming from without going too easy on you. They choose you to work with because you've shared similar purposes and goals in your lives. They work with many people at once. You also have a bunch of other guides with specific skills. As your circumstances change and/or your soul evolves, one guide may exit your life as another takes you on the next leg of your journey. New guides, with special abilities appropriate for these new stages, help you reach certain goals and overcome challenges. For the most part, they stay in the background until you need them, and they may be guiding others at the same time.

All guides help you by communicating with signs, symbols, and feelings. They're not always consistent in how they choose to help, since this may be part of the plan. Guides can stick around for a short or long time, depending on how long you need them. They're often the source of ideas that bring us focus and self-satisfaction—what a lot of people call "inspiration." And because you learn various lessons and have many needs at once, you can have many guides at the same time. You may have different guides for your career, family, ability to care for a sick friend, etc. Pat has one guide for teaching and a different one for healing, but because she does both at the same time, they're both available.

Okay, so I have two current guides that I'm aware of. One is a Native American whom I recognize when he shows me his sign, which is a headdress. I call him "Chief." He also acts as a mentor and source of companionship and reassurance to me; I know that when he comes to me a lot, it means that I'm about to move forward in my gift. As a medium, I'm never done learning, and when I feel Chief's company, I know I'm getting ready for an energy shift and will begin channeling a little differently. My guardian angel Solerna, whom I talked about earlier, also does double duty as my guide. I'm not sure how this works, but I believe she's an angel *and* my guide because when I call on my guides, she and Chief step forward. Could they have more specific names or even more jobs that I'm not aware of? Sure. But what matters most to me is that they give me divine direction when I desire and require it, and if they're helping out from the Other Side, that's more important to me than knowing exactly what they're called and when.

Chief and Solerna excel at different things. Chief is really good at showing me other people's guides, especially if they're Native American or if the person I'm reading is drawn to that culture in his or her own life. Chief's messages are mostly serious, disciplined, and structured—a little like Sitting Bull. I'm not sure why my guide is Native American, but I'm intrigued by that heritage. Pat thinks he may also be a male protector for me, which makes sense since I feel that lately, he's spent a lot of time making sure that people aren't taking advantage of my spirituality and draining all my energy. I also love owls, which symbolize wisdom and sacred knowledge in Native American culture. Do I look like someone who's very earthy? No way. But apparently my soul is. As for Solerna, she addresses more divine topics for me. On the show, I did a reading for a wonderful man who had cancer. It was Solerna who stepped forward to tell me that it was okay to talk about death with him, even though it's not something I usually discuss. Most people see me to find comfort from losing a loved one, but this man, because of his health, wanted to know what happens when we pass. Solerna told me it was okay to answer his questions as best I could, because he wasn't dying anytime soon.

The best way to connect with your guides is through meditation, prayer, or just sitting quietly and listening to the response of your inner voice, or as I like to say, your Jiminy Cricket. You can also contact your guides through hypnosis by a trained facilitator or a psychic whose gift is to specifically channel these entities. When you're in a relaxed but focused headspace, you'll frequently hear your inner Jiminy Cricket giving you advice or prompting what's right for you. These feelings aren't just a hunch. More often than not, they're the words of your wise guides, responding to your call. You can ask them for specific help, guidance, and reassurance as often as you want.

Always Within Reach: Your Loved Ones

If you get nothing else from this book, know this: your deceased loved ones are loving, guiding, and protecting you from the Other Side. I say this a lot, but you can't hear it enough. Here's another thing I find comforting: Spirit says that we will see our family and friends when we cross over and be together during future lives on earth. I hope you like your sister, because she's sticking around for eternity, in one way or another!

Though I've talked about big-name figures like the Blessed

Mother or Jesus making cameos during a session, the majority of the souls I channel for my clients are those of their deceased loved ones. Sometimes when you're watching the show, you'll notice repeat themes or commonalities between the messages they pass on. *There was nothing you could do to help. He was with you when you got married. She wants you to embrace life without the burden of fear or guilt. He no longer has health issues* . . . and so on. I'm not doling out the same condolences to everyone with a dead friend or family member, hoping to hit the bull's-eye eventually. No, no, no. Spirit has me deliver healing messages based on what the person is holding on to and needs to hear from their loved ones. So it's not that the message is generic or recycled, but that humanity shares similar struggles. It's a little like when you cry after hearing a popular song on the radio; you're not the only one who relates to the lyrics, but that doesn't make your reaction any less real. What's more, the stuff I mentioned above isn't how *everyone* responds to a death. Like for me, none of the things I said apply to the way I felt when my grandmothers passed. If anything, I wondered if they liked the dresses we buried them in, and now, I wonder what they think of our new bathroom and if they feel I'm working too hard!

And again, the souls that I channel are safe and at peace. A lot of movies, books, and TV shows talk about souls that are trapped between our world and the Other Side. I know there are mediums that work with, and help transition, these "stuck souls" into the light, but this isn't what I've felt called to do, so this isn't who I feel I'm connecting with. Mediums can communicate with the dead differently, and I prefer to channel souls that are already in Heaven. So if one *were* stuck, I wouldn't be the best person to tell!

Young and Well-Connected: Children and Babies

I hear from the souls of young people so often that I want to talk about them separately for a minute. The families that loved and cherished them feel unthinkable sorrow for their loss, but I'm not here to tell you that God never gives you more than you can handle blah blah blah. I want you to know that when I channel the souls of children and babies, they tell me they're in a good place and always with you. You'll also see them again; I guarantee it.

In the last chapter, I talked about what souls looked like—that the way Spirit presents themselves to me is either how we remember them or how they would like us to remember them. With kids, sometimes they'll come forward and say, "Tell my mom I'm on a swing set, wearing my favorite pink dress!" which causes the parent to say, "Oh my God, that's one of my favorite memories!" I'm not sure if the child literally plays on swings all day in a dress, or if this is a message the soul tells me to validate a special memory and bring her parents peace. Then again, I feel Heaven is a breathtaking place where anything is possible. People who've had near-death experiences report seeing lush, technicolor fields and sparkling pools of water; it's a place where souls sing and dance, and animals play. So who's to say there isn't the craziest jungle gym you've ever seen right in the middle of it. Maybe you get dibs on the slide if you wear a dress!

Souls do tell me that it's really important for us to know that your children's souls grow and evolve on the Other Side. I suspect this is what babies and kids are referring to when they show themselves to me as a small soul, and then as they approach me, they get bigger. I don't usually talk about soul development in a reading, because it's a bit long and involved, so I just tell the parents that they've "grown." Time is different in Heaven, and as I've said, I don't think souls age the way we do here because they don't have a physical body. So when they show themselves as a shadow but with gorgeous, wavy hair or sparkly blue eyes, I can't be certain but I imagine they're pointing these traits out for their loved ones' benefit because that's how they want to be, or are, remembered. Souls may also get to pick their age—one they feel the most comfortable being. And as I often say, the way Spirit shows itself also has to do with the message that will bring the person the most healing at that moment. So the same soul may appear one way to a skeptic who wants validation, another way to a return client who wants to connect, and still a third way to someone who is seeing me for the first time and is grieving. I've found that those who are the most anguished are the ones who want to know how old their child is or what it's doing in Heaven. They're the ones whose souls most commonly tell them about growth and swing sets.

Realize this too: children's souls know when, and are so grateful for how, you memorialize them. A woman came to me once because her daughter died at birth. I told her that her child's soul was telling me that her mom had her actual footprints tattooed on her, and that there was also something about butterflies . . . ? Turns out, the woman did have her daughter's little feet inked on the bottom of her leg, but *as* the body of a butterfly. Spirit said she did this in memory of her daughter, because the child's footprints were the only thing she had of hers. Rest assured that as often as your child is on your mind, you're in their thoughts too. You're connected by love. In fact, Spirit likes to show me a soul sitting in a chair, watching a parent from Heaven. Sometimes right after a little one dies, its soul will sit with a loved one's physical body for a bit.

I also channel a lot of miscarried, stillborn, and terminated souls. Miscarried souls are quick to appear at the start of a session, and stillborns channel phenomenally well. In fact, stillborn babies often describe how it felt if their mothers held them, how parents dressed them in certain articles of clothing, or if a mom wrapped her child's hand around her finger and studied every inch of her body. At a really large venue I announced that someone in the room had the actual footprints of a boy and girl with her who'd passed. A woman stood up and said she brought the prayer card for two of her children who'd died—she gave birth to triplets, and while her son survived, the two other babies didn't. One was a son, and the other was a daughter. There are also parents who don't get to hold their child after it passes, but these souls insist that they are still with their parents the whole time. I'm not sure if stillborn baby souls remember this stuff from their life here or are seeing it from the Other Side, or maybe a little of both. Like miscarried and stillborn souls, terminated souls haven't fulfilled their journeys, but they'll show me that they frequently reenter other bodies right away. They'll also tell me if the termination was part of a bigger lesson for someone still here in the physical world.

When we think about a child's life, many of us believe it begins at some point at, or after, conception. But a person's soul exists long before their body does. That's why Spirit can tell me so much about an impending pregnancy: the soul's been around and waiting to incarnate for a while. If you're pregnant, Spirit can tell me if the baby will be a girl or boy—a pink blanket is my sign for a female; a blue one for a male. If I see a flash of these signs, it usually means Spirit won't report the sex because the person might not want to know. If a woman doesn't know she's pregnant, I might feel like my stomach is expanding. Finally, if a family is adopting a baby, I can also tell that. If you're going to be a parent, to me, you're expecting. It doesn't matter how the child comes into your life.

A lot of times, a deceased loved one acknowledges that it held the soul of a baby before it came to the physical world. Spirit will validate this with something specific about the child at its birth, whether it's a crooked pinky, turned foot, dimple, or a birthmark or distinct marking on the back of its neck, arm, face, leg, or under its hair. This is Spirit's way of saying, *I know your baby so well that I can identify its most intimate details.* It's like the kiss of being.

It's also no secret that children are naturally more intuitive than most adults, and I think it helps that they are much closer to their soul's time in Heaven. I'll get into children's encounters with Spirit later, but I want to touch on this here because once in a while, kids who've crossed over see Spirit before they pass. It's as if they're still acutely aware of the continuum that travels from the Other Side, to this world, and back. One of the most touching examples of this is about a boy named Julien, who was diagnosed with AML leukemia at three and a half years old. He was just over eight when he died.

Julien's contact with Heaven reads like a who's who of Spirit. A month after his fourth birthday and first bone marrow transplant, Julien's family and doctors thought he was out of the woods, though he was about to relapse. This is when Julien began getting messages from God, through a female Spirit he later identified in a book as the Blessed Mother. There are two messages that Julien's mom knows of. The first occurred shortly after Julien's transplant, when he said, "Maman, I have something to tell you, but I'm afraid it will make you sad. God came to me in a dream and said I had to come back soon. He said my leukemia has returned and my time here is over." This was surprising news, since Julien's mom thought his transplant would help him recover. Not long after this dream, Julien heard from the Blessed Mother again, but this time, she was crying. She told him that when he died, his mom would be very sad but eventually be okay.

Two days later, Julien's doctor found abnormal cells from a bone marrow aspiration. Sure enough, the boy's dreams were prophetic. Julien's mom was devastated and prayed for a miracle. She took him to the shrine of St. Padre Pio in Pennsylvania. When she saw Julien holding the hand of, and whispering to, a Padre Pio statue in the gift shop, she bought it for him and put it in the backyard (Julien and his statue were the same height). Two months after their trip, Julien dreamed of a two-year-old boy who came to play with him and tell him about a conversation that God had with Padre Pio about Julien's future. Julien then asked the boy if he should follow him to Heaven, and at the time, the boy said that Julien was not ready. Julien's mom now believes the boy was actually an angel sent to bridge our world and Heaven for her son, when it was his time to go.

Julien's encounters with Spirit weren't limited to highly evolved souls. Every time he was in severely critical condition, he asked his mom if she could see "them" and looked toward the ceiling; he whispered to the sky a lot. When his mom worked up the nerve to ask who "they" were, he said one of the beings was his mom's friend Jackie, who died on 9/11. When she asked where Jackie was, he answered as if it were obvious: "Mommy, she is right there next to you." Jackie died before Julien was born; he'd never met her.

Julien and his mother did not discuss angels or God again,

until the weeks before he died. At that point, he told his mom he was scared to leave her, but she "had his heart," and he was going to "a beautiful place." Julien told her all the time that he chose her to be his mom, and that God pointed her out and said that if he selected her, she'd take care of him. He talked a lot about "one God for everyone." Julien's mom believes that her son was a gift, sent to help her and others believe in God and the afterlife. In the middle of the night recently, her niece awoke to a sparkling light in her room and an image of Julien's face, smiling, just inches from her own. He was with his mom's friend Jackie.

When I channeled Julien, he told me that his mom never treated him like he was sick and always made sure he was happy. She let him leave when it was time, and he said he had a beautiful passing. He could feel his mother's heart beating when his stopped.

Best Friends Forever: Animals

I don't know about you, but I'm crying over here. So after such a sad story, I want to end this chapter on a happier note. And what makes us smile more than our beloved animals?

People love their pets, and I've channeled cats, dogs, horses, birds, and even a fish (that last one didn't have much to say). I even channeled a man's deceased mom and their pet squirrel. Of course, when the mother brought the animal forward, I didn't think it was a squirrel, because who keeps that as a pet? Aren't they filthy and rabid? So I asked the son if they had a ferret, and he said no. Then the mother's soul says to me, "Tell my son I have Stevie with me." I passed it on, and the guy just about falls off his chair. Not only did they have a pet squirrel named Stevie growing up, but his cremations were on his sister's mantel next to his mother's! He also had a picture of his mom sitting on the sofa, feeding the little squirrel. The mom cooked for the rodent and everything.

You can probably guess that dogs and cats come forward most often, but that's just because more people keep them as pets than they do, say, squirrels. I may hear a dog walking on a wooden floor, or Spirit might show me that a client kept toys from the dog or how their pet died. They'll also tell me when the client made all the right choices about an end-of-life decision, so that the dog didn't suffer. My symbol for that is Gram's dog Lucky Girl, who became very ill from eating the berries from a poinsettia plant; though the vet thought she was poisoned from it, my grandmother took her home because she didn't appear to be suffering. She recovered and lived for many more years. But it doesn't take Spirit to bring animals forward; sometimes they'll come bounding through on their own. There've even been times when I've asked clients if they've lost a child, because I can feel the bond of a mother and son, though it's a bit more removed than that of a human bond, and it turns out that the person lost a dog they loved like a child. This happens a lot with cats too—cat people are really attached!

Like children, animals have a special relationship to Spirit. Their brains aren't as full as ours are, so they see and sense Spirit more easily than we do. The next time your cat seems to meow at nothing, or your dog's head looks like it's watching a rebounding pinball in the air, say hi to Spirit. My dogs are named Louis Vuitton and Peter James—and Petey is like a person. He talks to Spirit all the time; I call him the dog hunter of Spirit. He barks, mumbles, and makes bizarre noises, often while lying on the stairs with his head hanging over the edge. I think it's because energy hangs on my staircase. I sit with my back to it during readings, because I sense Spirit there. Is it like this in everyone's house? I don't know. But I've heard about dogs barking at landings a lot, and I just did a reading where a child saw Spirit on her stairs too. Anyway, when I do readings, I put the dogs in a separate room because Petey is a talker and Louis, a Yorkie, is very jittery and barks all the time at nothing. He can't sit still, so I think he senses Spirit. It's not like I see Spirit and then watch my dogs bark at it, because there's so much energy around me that I don't notice that kind of correlation. Louis also anxiously paces back and forth with his bone, like someone's going to take it from him. Spirit *has* been known to make things disappear. Poor Louis. That's one tricky game of fetch!

So, You Want to Connect
with Souls in Heaven?

I believe that everyone has the ability to communicate with Spirit and develop their intuition. I also think it comes more easily to some than others. Remember those old Barbizon ads that said, "Be a model . . . or just look like one"? I loved them! That tag line pops into my head whenever I hear a medium or book title imply that anyone can talk to dead people with the same accuracy and regularity that those of us with more developed, natural abilities do. The idea is so mainstream, in fact, that there are a bunch of wikiHow and eHow pages devoted to this on the Internet. I also think that when we open a connection to the Other Side to hear from Spirit or a loved one, there are ways to do this that are better than others, and I want to be sure you have safe, realistic expectations about your own abilities as you read. I don't want everyone to think that by the end of the chapter, you'll be able to shut your eyes, count to three, and when you open—presto!—you'll see Aunt Lisa standing in front of you. Not everyone can do it when they want. It *could* happen, but if not, I don't want you to doubt your bond or think your departed loved ones aren't around, because the opposite is true. They're with you all the time.

So if you want to open a connection with Spirit and loved ones who've crossed over, I feel the best way to do this is to use a few simple tools to help you become more aware of how Spirit is already with us every day. Meditating, listening to your gut, recognizing signs, identifying visitations in dreams—these are all ways that we receive messages from Spirit. If anything goes on around you that seems odd, weird, different, or a coincidence—and these things also make you think of a loved one or remind you of that person—please embrace it as a sign that the soul is with you at that exact moment. Also, I feel that the more you acknowledge these hellos from Heaven, the more you will receive. You share a bond with your loved ones that can never be broken, and I want you to know that they're just as interested in reaching out to you as you are to them. And no, you're not bothering them in any way. They *want* you to know they're with you, that they're helping you and that they're experiencing a beautiful existence beyond this one.

Once your mind is open, and you start to get validation that you're interacting with Spirit—maybe a dream here, a sign there—please don't get upset or discouraged if you can't do this all the time, or when you want to, or that your messages aren't as specific as you crave. Spirit has its own agenda—its own motives, rules, and timing for everything that happens to and around us. Remember how I said that during my sessions, Spirit delivers messages that people *need* to hear, not what they *want* to hear? Spirit's presence in your life is the same way. Don't hate me for saying it, but a lot of times having faith, trusting that there's a bigger plan, or simply not knowing is part of a lesson we're meant to learn. I also think that one reason we can all connect with Spirit to some degree is because we're meant to and should—for healing, support, intervention, and validation of our spiritual beliefs. And while expanding that intuitive part of ourselves is intended to benefit our own souls in all kinds of ways, we also can't forget that it's meant to help others too.

This leads me to what I think is really one of the most amazing and compelling reasons to develop your intuition, besides becoming aware of your loved one's presence. Not everyone is put on this earth to talk to dead people, but I feel that we are all here to learn service to others. So soon enough, you'll be able to connect with Grandma Betty in special ways, but you may also find that as your intuition grows, it leads you down other paths. As you become more aware of Spirit, you may also want to explore your intuition and spiritual connection more deeply. If so, you can read more on the topic or find a teacher or mentor to help you develop your own gifts. You might ultimately use your intuition not to become a medium, but a counselor who helps people with your insight, a facilitator who puts people in the right place, or a listener who always seems to be there when a person needs guidance. All of these roles rely on intuition that's made better by spiritual direction. This reminds me of a friend I have who is very gifted. She earns a six-figure income in a marketing and advertising job in Manhattan, and throughout her career, she's built relationships with her clients on a much more personal level. When they ask her for advice, it often comes from Spirit. Now, they don't *know* she leans on Spirit for help—only that she's wise beyond her years and always seems to know just what to say—but that's how this woman uses her gift. And like that, everyone wins.

Chuck Your Fear

As someone with a boatload of phobias, I'm no stranger to fear. But a huge part of connecting with the Other Side is having faith that what you're hearing and channeling is true and protected by God. Because here's the thing: you can't have both faith *and* fear as dominant factors in your life. The two contradict each other, they're opposing forces. So in order to connect with Spirit, you have to lose the fear and embrace the faith. I know that for me, the day I released any fear about being a medium, when I accepted that what I was doing was real and I wasn't insane, is when my life became a lot easier. Replacing fear with faith is a good rule to live by in any aspect of your life, really. New jobs, relationships, even asking for a loan from your parents . . . they're all made better when you lead with trust than when you go into them riddled with doubt and worry.

Another reason why you don't want to be afraid when you try to connect with Spirit is that it's not practical. I hate wasting time, don't you? Well, when you're scared, positive spiritual activity happens less often. But if you let Spirit know you're not afraid to see or hear them, doors fly open. I realize that it can be a totally freaky thing to hear a voice or see a figure standing near your bedroom door. Though I talk to Spirit all the time, it still startles me every once in a while too. What might help is if you first imagine what it would be like if this happened, so that if it ever does, you'll be less afraid. Maybe you can lie in bed and pretend Grandpa Wally is standing at the foot of it, or sit in the dining room and imagine him speaking to you from across the table. This will help normalize the experience and welcome your loved one, if you ever have an encounter like this. Will this type of visualization tip make Spirit visit faster? It may, but the bigger point is for you to not ruin your pants if Spirit shows up unannounced!

The final reason why you shouldn't embrace fear is, by far, the most important of all. Are you paying attention? Okay. So I do *not* mess with negative Spirit, but I was taught that anybody can open a not-nice doorway to the Other Side, and fear both attracts and feeds negativity. I want nothing to do with negativity and neither should you. Examples of how fear breeds negativity aren't just limited to Spirit; it's a life lesson too. I know a woman who is dyslexic, and it took years for her teachers and doctors to diagnose her learning disability. Every time she took a test at school, she'd feel afraid that she'd fail and it would make her feel stupid. She'd get down on herself because of her fear, so by the time she took the actual exam, she wasn't just scared of failing, she also hated the stupid test, and her dumb school, and her ugly teacher . . . You see how worry fed her negativity, and things went downhill? Similarly, when you're increasing awareness of Spirit, you have to stay positive to keep away any chance of interacting with negativity.

And if I've said it once, I'll say it a million more times: *no Ouija boards*. With these devices, you can call in whatever Spirit and energy is out there and available, and there's a good chance you'll channel an energy that will be sneaky and not benefit you in any way. You do not want these souls in your life.

Spiritual Bubble Wrap: Seek Protection and Grounding

Meditation is the best way to open to Spirit or a loved one that has crossed. It quiets your mind and helps you listen to your guides and communicate with Spirit, but you *must* ground and protect yourself in God's white light first. Some people like to picture themselves in an egg- or circle-shaped bubble, which is great, but I visualize the outline of my body in white light—for lack of a better metaphor, like the chalk drawing at a crime scene. I also visualize all gray negativity leaving my physical, emotional, and spiritual body and being replaced with pure, white light.

If during meditation you ask to hear from a loved one, you *must* do the same and say that you will only communicate with souls that walk in God's light. I don't want to hear that you're connecting with what are called low-level energies, which are easily accessed souls that have attained the least amount of awareness and growth. They are also the souls of people who were psychotic, had no remorse for criminal actions, and did other sketchy things in the physical world. Low-level energies are what corrupt corner psychics and crooked tarot card readers channel. These psychics are intuitive, but if they're also con artists and thieves, they've likely been raised from when they were young to get information the easiest way possible—which is from low-level energy. They don't care where their material comes from, the way I and other balanced mediums do. They only want enough to draw you in, from whatever or whoever will give it to them.

To be honest, I surround myself with God's light even when I'm not about to meditate. I do it first thing in the morning during my prayers to keep negativity away all day. I also do it if I'm nervous, like when I have a meeting about work or I'm about to speak in front a group of people for a charity. I like to do it if I'm going to take a flight as well. I envision the plane, pilot, and staff in a bubble of radiant light to keep us safe from harm.

After I ask God to surround me in His white light and protection, I then ground myself to the earth. I do this before a reading and before I meditate, which is how I open to Spirit. I was taught to ground myself by imagining two cords from the bottoms of my feet, and one from my tailbone, shooting into the earth and locking them in like the roots of a tree. If you don't ground and protect yourself prior to meditating, any energy level can walk right in, or you can become depleted or take on another soul's energy. I then ask that all information I receive be for the highest good of all concerned, I ask for God's guidance, and I ask for unique validation during each reading. I then visualize God's light, as I begin to see my guides and the silhouettes of various souls lined up and waiting to speak, like that scene at the end of *Ghost,* where Patrick Swayze goes to Heaven.

Focus, People, Focus: How to Meditate

Meditation is the only way I can calm my mind, at any point in a day. When I'm quiet and focused, I can also hear what Spirit has to say. You can be quiet when you're praying too, but prayer is talking to God, whereas meditation lets you listen to God and other souls. I'll get into prayer more in chapter six, when we talk specifically about Him.

There's no right or wrong place to meditate. I can connect with Spirit anytime, anywhere—well, okay, maybe not while getting frisky with Larry. But a quiet room in your house, on the beach, in the bathtub, at the park . . . wherever you feel safe and peaceful is as good a place as any. You can find self-guided meditations online or on iTunes to help you feel grounded, balanced, and receptive to Spirit as well. You can also sit in a quiet room for twenty minutes by yourself to clear your head. By meditating, you won't just open yourself up to Spirit either. You'll also learn *how* you connect—whether it's through feeling, smell, sight, and so on, because Spirit will come through most vividly using your choice senses. You might see a film strip, or a figure standing in your mind's eye. Or you may hear or feel a voice say just one healing word or an entire calming sentence. You might even experience a combination of a few senses, which is very common too.

If meditating sounds too out-there for you, know that Spirit can also come to you when your head is off in la-la land and you're daydreaming, which is similar to the relaxed state you go into when you meditate. I get the most information from Spirit when I'm in the shower and when I blow-dry my hair—and I don't think it's because Spirit likes the scent of my shampoo and styling cream (though it does smell like chai tea). I am, however, starting to think it's true when they say, "The higher the hair, the closer to God!" Other people I know are most receptive to Spirit when they're doing a boring chore like vacuuming or washing the dishes. These are the moments when your mind's not cluttered with a to-do list of activities and is naturally open to hear from Spirit. And yes, they can talk over the roar of your Hoover!

Beyond connecting with your loved ones, meditation and prayer are also helpful in my everyday life. I don't need to be about to channel to benefit. Praying and meditating help me feel balanced, grounded, and safe at all times. God, angels, guides, loved ones who've passed, and even souls we haven't met in Heaven are guiding and protecting us always. Given what I do, I'd be a real schmuck if I didn't connect with them now and again, and in prayer, tell them how grateful I am for all their hard work.

A few other tips that work for me and may do the same for you: as I meditate, I like to visualize the aligning of my chakras (you can find helpful diagrams online of where these are on your body) and picture them filling up with pure, white light. I also try to keep my body cleansed by not using drugs or alcohol, or eating too poorly, otherwise it confuses my energy and messes with my ability to connect with Spirit. In addition to meditation, I find that drum circles help me connect with various souls, as well.

Make Like a Seventies Song, and Read the Signs

One reassuring way that Spirit likes to communicate is by sending signs to show they're near. This requires no preparation on your part—it just happens. Spirit already does this, but we tend to get so bogged down by our lives that we may not notice. These signs may come when you need them most, or as a surprise. The key is to know what to look for.

So you know how doctors say you should always call them if you have symptoms out of the ordinary for your body—something that's not your idea of normal? A slightly high temperature, for instance, might be normal for one person, but to another, it could be the start of the flu. It's that way with Spirit too. If you get a sign you're not accustomed to seeing—a situation that's not normal for you—I've found that it's likely a symbol or sign from your loved ones that they're with you at that exact moment. Some of the more typical signs I hear about are seeing random feathers, loose change, animals, insects, and religious articles. Numbers are also a way that Spirit connects with us. For example, seeing the sequence 1-1-1 means that divine intervention's happening, or about to. When I see the numbers 6-0-9, the day Gram died, I know she's with me at that moment. Gram also leaves dimes all around me. I've found them randomly in the bottom of my makeup bag or one might fly out of my wallet—no joke. Victoria even found one at a gymnastics meet. She was in her leotard, and when she sat down on the mat, she felt something cold stuck to her bare leg. It was a dime, and I think Gram was wishing her good luck.

As a medium, I've also learned that if you don't have a lot of strict expectations about how a loved one "should" connect with you, it will be easier for that soul to do so. I'm not saying that you need to accept any random occurrence as a sign; that's just silly and naïve. But sometimes, we close ourselves off from connecting because of nitpicky limits we put up. For example, at a small group reading in Long Island, a woman told me that she smells gardenias a lot, but that it couldn't be *her* mother because her mom's favorite flower was lily of the valley. Seriously? Another woman I know says that she smells shampoo at odd times, but that it couldn't be *her* mother's soul reaching out to her, because she was known for her Rave hair spray. When I hear this stuff, it makes me nuts. Because here's the thing: Spirit doesn't always send signs that exactly match up to our expectations or memories, but they're usually in the ballpark. I don't know why these souls don't nail it, but what matters in these examples is that the women's moms were regularly reaching out in ways that were uncommon so they'd get noticed. But because their daughters were so literal, they missed the wonderful reunions. I get why mother-daughter relationships can be full of misunderstandings in the physical world, but jeez, these moms now live in another dimension. Cut the women some slack!

Just as mediums connect with Spirit in different ways, you do too. When people experience Spirit differently, it's because of what *we're* able to see and feel, not because of how *Spirit* chooses to communicate with that person. This is why a husband can see Spirit at the end of the bed, but his wife, right beside him, cannot. I had a client say to me, "My sister dreams of my brother, so that must mean he's not with me or visiting me." But dreams were simply the way that this one sister connected with Spirit. The client's brother may have been trying to reach her through butterflies or the sudden smell of his cologne, and either she'd missed the signs because she was stuck on dreaming, or she hadn't opened up yet in a way that he could reach her. A lot of people also ask me if you should set up a system with your loved ones while they're still alive—*Come back as a frog! Move the frames in our house!*—and I think that's a cute idea. But if the soul can't do that, or you don't interpret signs that way, you're out of luck if it never happens.

The thing is, Spirit always shows up on its own. You just need to trust your instincts to know what's unusual and meaningful, and what's not. At a venue in Atlanta, I channeled a woman's son who was in a car accident. She was raw, devastated, and angry. The boy's soul had me ask if his mom ever finds white feathers in odd places, and when she said she did, a tiny piece of white tissue confetti paper floated down from the ceiling. Nobody knew where it came from; she wasn't even seated under the balcony! We captured the whole thing on camera too. But imagine if the woman were so stuck on feathers that she dismissed this feather-*like* object altogether? She'd have ignored a spectacular moment that let her know that her son was listening to her and always beside her, especially when she was grieving in such a sensitive and distressing way.

I particularly love when Spirit sends signs that make us laugh. I know a woman who lost her husband to cancer at a young age. A year later, she was in Miami with her friends during a much-needed girls' weekend. They were lying on the beach, when she began talking about her mother-in-law. She was saying that it had been a hard relationship to negotiate without her spouse, since each woman dealt with losing the son/husband differently. Well, right in the middle of this, a seagull pooped on the wife's arm. I have a hunch it was her husband's soul telling her, *Stop gossiping about my mom, already!*

Oh, here's something else you should know: when Spirit gives you a sign, it doesn't mean that the soul *is* that sign—that is, the husband's soul was not the seagull (or the poop). Spirit uses these objects to get your attention and let you know they're around. When Pat's father passed, she'd never seen a cardinal on her property in thirty years. Her dad died in mid-February, and within a few weeks the first cardinal presented itself as she was helping her mom into the car to go to church. There were no leaves on the trees yet, but it started chirping loudly right on a branch above her. After that, she saw a cardinal at her house, or wherever she was, on a daily basis. There was one on her windowsill, the patio, at the graveyard on Easter . . . Her mom passed away the following June, and don't you know, a female cardinal began accompanying the male almost immediately? The two would sit together in a tree in her yard. How incredible is that? But Pat's parents aren't the lovebirds she saw. Their souls were using the cardinals to bring her peace.

Beyond birds, insects are also common signs—mostly pretty butterflies, dragonflies, or ladybugs that make you think, *Aww. I miss you too, Cousin Sarah!* And then there's my Nanny, who comes to my family as a big, fat, ugly housefly with hair sticking out all over—you know, those enormous ones you see maybe twice a year. Except I see them all the time, no matter where I am or what season it is. The way I interpret Nanny coming back as a fat fly is that she was Italian, and when she died, she was seventy-six pounds; but as this insect, she's plump and letting it all hang out. It also means she can zip around us all she wants! Nanny died in January and though most houseflies live during warmer months, Nanny's flies thrive year-round. On the day she passed, I remember seeing the fly on a lamp in the house, which I found strange. Then right after, I saw a huge fly at the funeral home, then I saw one in my bathroom, and on it went. Once I went to a nerve-racking meeting on the twentieth floor of a New York City skyscraper and a huge fly started buzzing in my face. The windows didn't open, so how did the fly get up there? Did it take the elevator? I even saw Nanny during my very first meeting for this book. She was in the mirror behind my cowriter Kristina while we were having lunch!

Since I've established that Nanny's an enormous fly, she shows up all the time for support, especially for the bigger milestones. The funniest story about this happened after I gave birth to my daughter, Victoria. It was one a.m., I wasn't feeling well, and a nurse stuck her head into my room to see if she could get me something to eat. I said sure, I'd take anything. So I'm thinking that she'd bring me Jell-O at the most, and she comes back with a big tray, and on it was a covered dish. When the nurse lifted the silver top, it wasn't lobster. There was a big, fat fly sitting on top of a salad! It was disgusting, but it made me cry. Nanny wanted me to know she was with me during her great-granddaughter's birth, and while I felt ill. I also don't think she'd have wanted me to eat a salad, so her energy encouraged a fly to land on top of it! I asked the nurse for some pasta instead.

When deceased loved ones like Nanny or Gram want me to pass on a message to a family member, I don't do it outright, the way I do with my clients or people I see when I'm out and about; I ask Spirit to guide us to signs instead. It happened during the episode we filmed where we bought art for Victoria's dorm room with the lyrics to "You Are My Sunshine" painted on it. Gram used to sing that song all the time. Seeing this sign meant the world to me and V, since I sensed this was Gram's way of saying she'd watch over Victoria. What the show didn't air was that a big, fat fly flew right into the cameraman's mouth while we were filming, so Nanny was there too!

After you've opened yourself up to getting signs, don't hesitate to ask for one if you need it for support or encouragement. Your loved ones don't always get *right* back to you—they usually wait until the time is right—but when they do, their gestures will knock your fishnets off. I know a woman named Anna whose mom had just died, and while she was working at her computer, she felt a wave of sadness from missing her. She said out loud, "Mom, I wish I could feel you kiss my cheek again." Just then, Anna was overcome with chills, which caused her to grab a sweater that her mom had left at the house. She put her hands in the pockets to warm them and found a neatly folded tissue with a perfect outline of her mom's lips on it. Anna's mother always wore red Revlon lipstick and would blot her mouth once before going out. The woman put the red lip marks against her cheek and felt so much better. Anna's mom sent her the sign she needed.

So what do you do when you get a sign from a loved one? Say hi, tell the soul that you miss him or her, share how you feel, fill them in on any news from your life, and/or just say, "I love you." You don't need to have a long conversation. Simply acknowledging Spirit's presence is enough. But don't get so hung up on looking for signs that it consumes your day. Like that old cliché about love, Spirit can come to you when you least expect it. Simply ask for a sign or visit, and then release it with faith.

Who Moved My Keys?

Another way that Spirit and your loved ones like to get in touch is by manipulating things in and around your home. They'll tilt pictures, move objects, turn the water on in the sink, turn electrical appliances on and off, make objects go missing, and cause your pets to behave strangely. You may also hear knocking, footsteps, or dishes clanging around in the kitchen. All of these things require a lot of energy from Spirit, so they're working very hard to get you to notice them if you experience this! And if Spirit is very close to you, you might feel chills, pressure in your ears, or a tingly sensation in your head. Spirit might even touch you, or direct your attention to someone who looks exactly like a loved one, then a minute later, not at all. This is why you might feel like you saw your dead godmother in the grocery store, but when you looked back, she was different or gone. Or here's one I get all the time—for a brief moment when your pet gives you a certain look or acts a particular way, he resembles a person in your life who has passed away.

Manipulating electrical equipment is one of the easiest ways for Spirit to announce they're with you because they, too, are made of energy. I know a woman whose husband bought a metal, industrial-style lamp from a store in SoHo years ago, before he died from melanoma. It was very much his style, and he really loved it. The man's wife's aunt was with him when he made the purchase, and during the family's first Christmas without him, she was telling the story about when they bought the piece. Halfway through the anecdote the lamp turned off, and a few seconds later it turned back on again. Not only did this soul manipulate electricity, but he also chose a meaningful way to do it!

Of all the electrical equipment that Spirit could finagle for me—lamps, TVs, stoves, lights, hair dryers, irons—it often prefers to play with the cameras around me. When I was on tour in Philadelphia, I did a reading in an old theater. We were having a great time, so Pat took out her iPhone to snap some photos, but the camera began taking them on its own! When I looked at the pictures, I saw a little girl peeking out from behind Larry's leg and my team was covered in huge blue orbs. This last part didn't surprise me because Spirit typically appears in photos as a blue haze, orb, or streak, or as a white, smoky cloud or streak. Sometimes if you zoom in on an orb, you can even see the image of a face. I've also seen little orange lightning bolts over my head.

In photos, souls can also appear as people, which can be confusing. About three years ago, my family threw a party at a restaurant, and someone took a picture of me and my cousins. In the shot, we're all blurry, but between me and my cousin Lisa, you can distinctly see her uncle, dressed in a leisure suit, who died in a motorcycle accident thirty-five years prior. Also in the picture is a profile of St. Teresa and my deceased great-uncle wearing big sunglasses. What kind of motley crew is St. Teresa hanging out with? My sister-in-law Corrinda even has a picture where the Blessed Mother's silhouette is facing her. (She had no idea what she was marrying into.) Of course, everyone always says it's because of me that our family photos turn out so weird. But this doesn't just happen to me. Pat's father showed himself in two Labor Day photos—one, in a flame directly above her brother's head in which her dad's facial features were clearly discernible, and in another, where he appeared more as a hologram. If you look back at photos of your own celebrations or family gatherings, you may see an orb or image that surprises you too!

Spirit also likes to fool around with toys, especially if it has a special meaning or is easy to manipulate. When I was in Long Beach, California, I read for two grandparents whose granddaughter had died, and her soul showed me my sign for a soul setting off toys in the house. When I asked them if this happened, the family couldn't place it. So the soul upped its game for a clearer message. She said to me, "Tell them about my *tricycle*"—and wouldn't you know, the grandparents kept the child's bike in their house, even after she died, and frequently heard the bell on it ringing. I can't tell you the number of times people tell me that their toys turn on without batteries, dolls fall off shelves, or that a Transformer's blue eyes glow in the middle of the night. In the dark, that last one sounds pretty creepy, but try to think of it as your loved ones saying good night.

I Dreamed a Dream

Spirit calls the time that we sleep our "teaching hours," since our mind is at rest and most easily accessible for them to pass on any guidance or information that we might need. So it makes sense to me that one of the easiest and most common ways that Spirit can communicate with us is when we're snoozing—either in a dream or visitation that feels like a dream. I don't dream of Spirit (or much, really), but a lot of my clients do, and there seems to be some confusion over the difference between a dream and a visitation. Let me try to explain the difference, because there can be some overlap.

Visitations from Spirit are brief, the messages are succinct, and then the moment's over. It may include a quick exchange, a few sentences, or just a word. Sometimes a loved one might stand there without talking, or the meaning is understood without words since souls communicate through thought. You'll remember the message (unlike how dreams are spotty the next day), and it will be clear as a bell. I've had many clients whose friends or family members appeared only long enough for a hug, and then disappeared. During a visitation, the person's presence is so vivid, it seems real. A friend told me a story about how she was adopting a baby from Ethiopia and was concerned that she didn't ask for enough medical tests to be run before she brought the child home. That night while she was sleeping, she saw the faces of her deceased aunt and uncle standing side by side, smiling, looking right at her. "Don't worry," they said. "Your daughter's health will be fine." Their mouths didn't move—they spoke telepathically, as souls do. It was over in seconds, and then she woke up. I assured her that this was, in fact, a visitation.

Visitations aren't always meant to comfort; they can also be a warning. I had a client whose deceased father came to her during a nap. She heard him speak into her ear, but in her mind, she framed it as if they were talking on the phone. The woman had a teenage daughter at the time who was acting very cagey. Her father told her to ask her daughter what was going on, and if she didn't share, to tell her that her Popsi said to. That was it. The woman woke up, went to her daughter's bedroom, and said, "Is there something you need to talk to me about? Popsi just—" Without another word, the girl began to cry. She said that she'd had sex for the first time that week, and the condom broke. She worried that she might be pregnant. The woman took her daughter to her first gynecologist appointment, and she was completely healthy and not pregnant. But it was a conversation that needed to happen, and they had Popsi to thank for it.

Now, dreams, on the other hand, can be long, rambling, creative, and elaborate; they're usually a jumble of thoughts, images, ideas, and feelings that need to be analyzed to be understood. They may reflect your emotions, wishes, or things that happened during the day. But Spirit's told me that you can also have visitations *within* a dream. Some mediums disagree with this, but I'm not so black-and-white with this stuff. Spirit is constantly surprising me. For instance, I had a client who welcomed visitations from her Nana after our first reading and received a few messages from her since. One night, she dreamed that her Nana hadn't died, but she didn't know it, and she realized that she'd missed out on the chance to spend meaningful time with her. In the dream, the woman found her Nana just sitting in her apartment, waiting for her. Nana had a warm and loving but very still demeanor, which is common in visitations. She didn't say a word; she just sat there long enough for her to give her a hug. Then the woman woke up. She and her Nana were close, so the girl never felt guilty that she wasn't there for her grandmother when she was alive; this wasn't her mind working things out in a dream. When my client told me about this, she said she didn't think it could be a visitation because some mediums say that you either dream or have a visitation—it's either one or the other, not both. But when she said this, her Nana's soul actually came through for us and confirmed that her experience was, in fact, a visitation within a dream.

Nana's soul also told me what the dreamlike visitation meant. "Her soul's been with you all this time, but you're doing so many more things together since you're open—thinking of her, including her in your life," I said. "She's obviously dead but her soul is very much alive and with you. She's saying, 'Look at all the time we can spend together!'" So don't be quick to dismiss a mixed-up dream if your loved one makes a cameo. You might not remember anything else from the dream—nothing may even make sense—but if their presence is visitation-like, it could very well be their soul saying hi.

Most visitations require little, if any, interpretation, but there are exceptions to this rule.

One last point: if you're grieving a loss or feeling guilt connected to a death, your negative feelings may lead you to believe that a visitation is heavier than it's meant to be. Say you dream of a loved one standing still for a split second, and the person doesn't say anything. You might even call out to him, but the image fades away. This is a typical visitation, but if you're carrying negative emotions related to the death, you may interpret it to mean that the person's soul is mad at you or didn't want to talk to you, and chose not to stick around for long. But that's never Spirit's aim at all! As you've just learned, visitations are special, well-intentioned, and yet another sign that a soul is at peace.

Intuition, Coincidence, Synchronicity—Oh My!

Do you ever get thoughts, feelings, or emotions that spring up in your head throughout the day, and you don't know where they come from? Have you ever felt confused, and when your intuition kicked in with the right solution, you thought, *Deep down in my soul, I just knew that job/man/house/college wasn't for me.* Maybe your gut said to turn down a date because something felt off, or to call your mom, who really needed to hear your voice. A lot of times, that's Spirit, including your guides and loved ones, giving you those messages, hunches, and inklings.

Coincidence is another gift from Spirit. I like to think of it as a wink from the Other Side that they're aware of our desires and doing their best to help and support us. How many times have you considered buying a new car, and suddenly you see your favorite model at every stoplight in town, which helps you make a smart choice? I remember wanting a very sparkly pair of shoes, and then seeing the best pair in one store window after the next, until I finally bought them (see the cover of this book!). These moments are Heaven-sent proof that Spirit's all ears, even if the coincidence involves something as ridiculous or frivolous as a car or shoes.

I think some of the most fun and significant coincidences happen through music. It's like when you're feeling down or confused, and then you hear a relevant song on the radio, and it's not even a Top 40 hit. The tune may be your loved one's favorite song, one you danced to at your wedding, or its lyrics may make your heavy heart feel lighter than it did all day. You happened to turn the radio on, to that station, at that exact moment—and yes, Spirit's behind it all. At a venue in Atlantic City, I did a reading for a teenager whose good friend died, and he was understandably devastated. When I channeled the boy, I said, "He's singing this song to me, and you probably don't even know it because you're so young. It's Billy Joel's 'Only the Good Die Young.'" The kid told me that on his way over, he'd heard that song, and it reminded him of his friend! Not only did his friend's soul urge him to turn the song on, but it was with him as he listened to it.

Some say there's music in Heaven, and Spirit likes to use the phrase "I'm singing with the angels now." So there's a connection between music and the afterlife that is very powerful. Spirit also says that music raises your vibration and brings your soul closer to God. Gram's favorite song was the 1930s classic "Dream a Little Dream of Me." Shortly after her death, I heard it *everywhere*. When it came on out of the blue at Bertucci's, which is not a quiet restaurant, it blasted out of the speakers and over the roar of the crowd. My whole family was like, *Did the music just come on? Why is this song so loud?* And what are the odds that Gram's song would play in Bertucci's? I don't think it's a typical Italian tune like "Volare" or "Tu Vuò Fà L'Americano."

Another amazing way that Spirit talks to us is with synchronicity. This is very similar to coincidence, but it's when two or more events that seem unrelated come together in a meaningful way. It's a special sign that grabs your attention and gives you proof that you're exactly where you're supposed to be on your spiritual path. During the first year after I accepted my gift and had just started my business, I walked past a booth full of Christmas ornaments. One was a sand dollar with the words "Merry Christmas, Theresa!" painted on it. It also had the year, with the words "Grandma loves you," and a picture of a child who, I swear to God, looks just like me. I took that as a sign that Nanny was saying, *You're on the right path. Don't worry, I'm here for you. I'm guiding you, I'm protecting you.* I thought I was doing the right thing, but I believe God and Nanny wanted me to know this too. Synchronicity doesn't happen as often as everyday coincidences, so it's powerful when it does. Another awesome example of this happened to my cowriter, when we were writing this chapter, actually. She's adopting a baby and often thinks of her future child when she hears a certain song on the radio. It isn't that popular, so when it does come on, it feels like a special surprise. One morning, she was outside and heard the prettiest music and realized it was coming from her iPhone. Her favorite song was playing through her Pandora app, though she didn't turn it on and never saved the song to her phone. In fact, she'd just been on her text message screen, so it would have taken at least four swipes or taps to even get to a station that may have played the tune. That's synchronicity! Spirit was telling her to be patient, because she's where she's supposed to be and they're helping to move things along at the right pace.

What Makes One Spirit Stronger Than Another?

Though Spirit tells me that everyone gets the messages they're meant to, I understand why it might feel frustrating or disappointing if friends or relatives seem to receive stronger Spirit communication than you do, either on their own or with a medium. I'm not talking about how limited awareness or preconceptions about how Spirit "should" communicate can hinder things—we covered that. I'm referring to the actual strength and clarity of the messages themselves. It's a fair question to ask, and I'll admit that in a group, or even privately, some souls communicate stronger, longer, and/or with more specificity than others can. So what gives? Here's what I've experienced.

Soul communication is influenced by various factors. Sometimes a soul might not have the energy to speak as much, or for as long, as a more developed soul can; it may even come in and out during a session, while others stay the whole time. As you know, souls are made up of energy—so think of how a 100-watt lightbulb shines brighter than a 45-watt bulb because it has more juice. One thing that determines a soul's energy is soul growth. The more a soul evolves here and in Heaven, the stronger it can communicate with us. More mature souls also give more detailed messages, because of soul growth. Finally, the more *you* heal here without your loved one, the stronger the soul's communication. To us, this may feel like the more time that's passed, the better the soul communicates, but there's more going on than that. And like I said, more advanced souls may strongly come through right away, which to us just feels inconsistent.

Another factor is how open you are to hearing certain messages. I've had people say to me, "I've been seeing mediums for ten years, and they've never brought up that topic. You're the best!" But this has nothing to do with me. It's about how well your loved ones can communicate and how receptive you are to receiving a message. You may not have been ready to hear a certain message five or ten years ago, or Spirit may have needed to learn certain lessons in that time to be able to communicate this information to you. Also, the more walls you put up, the harder Spirit has to work to validate its presence. I can deliver more messages, at a faster rate, if your loved ones don't need to keep reaffirming that it's really them. Staying positive about the messages you hear also helps. If you're not re-laxed, there isn't a positive flow of energy going on between us.

Managing expectations also comes into play here. If you expect to hear from a specific person—say, Aunt Jennie comes through instead of Uncle Charlie during a reading—or you want to get signs from your angels instead of a grandfather you never knew, that may be a problem. The quicker you accept that you'll get the message you need, from whomever you need to hear it from, the better the message will be. It's the message Spirit intended to de-liver from the start.

Some mediums say there's a transition period that can occur with a particularly difficult death, like a long-suffering disease or trauma, or when a loved one isn't ready to go, and this may cause a delay in hearing from the loved one. This isn't in my frame of reference, since I believe our souls are limitless, and that whatever you put forward to your guides is what you will receive. Because I've never personally experienced a time frame that Spirit's called a transition period, I have no reason to get into that with Spirit. File that under the ol' "I'll find out when I get there" category.

I've also found that readings are more informative if someone is particularly spiritual or intuitive themselves. This is also because Spirit doesn't have to work so hard with these people. Their read-ings embrace all the factors I just mentioned—they're open, they get it, they're healing well, their loved ones' souls tend to evolve at a good rate, et cetera.

One of the most incredible readings I did was for a woman named Kristy who came to a small group at her cousin's house. Her friend Jen, a teacher, had died at thirty-four years old and came through for us loud and clear. She talked about a note Kristy tucked into the side of her coffin when she was buried, about a mutual friend's wedding, Kristy's recent divorce, and even Kristy's cute new haircut. She then showed me that Kristy's lungs were pink, and that color is my sign for when a body part is newly healed. At that point, Kristy told us she'd recently undergone a successful double lung transplant for cystic fibrosis. Jen also talked about how Kristy felt unnecessarily guilty about her life-saving surgery, because Jen and some of their friends had died from the same disease. Jen's soul then told me to tell Kristy how proud she is that Kristy speaks about cystic fibrosis and advocates for organ donation, and at Kristy's most recent talk at a nursing convention for CF, at the center they both attended for care, Jen's soul said that she *and Kristy's lung donor* were there for it! Jen then brought Kristy's donor forward, who told us she'd donated everything on her body, including her eyeballs. She also told me Kristy would have children (which Jen had already told her in a dream), and brought through a mutual friend named Christina who died waiting for a transplant. Christina thanked Kristy for helping to take care of the daughter she left behind.

Up to this point, Kristy experienced a very moving reading, and it happened as quickly, fluidly, and accurately as you just read it above. And as if all those messages weren't powerful enough, Jen *then* told me that Kristy dreamed she went to Heaven and back—which Kristy confirmed. "I had a dream where Jen took credit for my surgery, and I was hovering above my body and watched the whole thing for a few minutes," Kristy said. "It felt very warm and comfortable, and I remember feeling disappointed when I woke up. I saw a few of my other friends who've died from CF too, in Heaven. They were together." The reading presented one sensational, crystal-clear detail after another.

So why was Kristy's reading so impressive? For one, there was a lot to be said! And I sensed that Kristy's soul was open and sensitive to Spirit already. I didn't need to spend much time validating Jen's presence—I got right to delivering messages about her life and what she needed to hear from her friend. Jen's energy was also very strong, so her points came across easily. The back-and-forth was amazing. It was like getting a strong Wi-Fi connection that lets you watch YouTube videos without waiting for them to buffer!

Setting Healthy Boundaries, Spirit Style

After a reading, clients have told me that they become more aware of Spirit's messages and signs. They may begin to see license plates, signs on trucks, number sequences, or hear specific messages in a song that either relates to them or a loved one who's departed. They might also have more intense visitations when they're sleeping. Acknowledge when these things happen and believe in them; you know a wow-moment when you have one. Take what occurred with my booking agent Rich. I read him during our first meeting, and his father's soul told me to mention cigars as validation—Dad loved a good stogie. For four months after, Rich couldn't escape the heavy scent of cigar smoke in his apartment. He regularly turned to his fiancée, Michele, in the middle of the night and said, "Can you believe someone's smoking a cigar at three in the morning?"

But Michele didn't smell anything. Then he'd run out to his terrace and even talk to neighbors, sure that he'd find the smoker, but he never did. The smell even followed him around during the day—in his car, office, and at the gym. Eventually, Rich came to embrace the smell as a sign from his father, and when he gets a whiff, he uses it as a cue to tell him what's going on in his life.

Because we all have souls around us that comfort and guide us, it can be simple to tap into them in the ways I've mentioned. Some of my clients think Spirit has to make a grand entrance—as an apparition, a winged angel over the bed, a vision while they're saying their prayers—yet this is rarely the case. That said, Spirit *can* come on a little strong sometimes. As you know, when I first started channeling Spirit in a deliberate way, I had to set boundaries about when they could communicate with me and what they'd look like. You may want to do the same thing. You're in control. If you notice that your dog is feeling harassed or you aren't sleeping very well, it's okay to say to Spirit, "I know you're here, but please don't show yourself to me or the pooch." Or, if you only want signs during the day but not at night, or to see Spirit but not feel them, tell them that. Get as specific as you want, but please, don't be afraid. If it feels like too much at some point, or even physically uncomfortable, you can also say, "By the grace of God, be gone," or just, "Please stop freaking me out." Be direct, and they'll respect your space.

A lot of people ask me if after communicating with Spirit, you'll feel depleted or exhausted because souls need your energy to communicate; this happens a lot on ghost-hunting shows. But this doesn't happen to me. Especially after large shows, I'm actually wound up and energized. I feel rejuvenated when I talk to Spirit, and I think that's because I ground myself first. If anything, *not* reading the energy drains me; it can make me feel anxious, so it's a release when I get the message out. Also, I only communicate with souls who walk in God's light, so the vibration of this energy is higher and lighter.

Kids Who See Dead People

Since our minds need to be clear for Spirit to communicate with us—the way it is during meditation, prayer, and sleep—this is one reason we hear about so many young people talking to souls who've crossed. Their minds are open and carefree. They don't worry about paying bills, scheduling carpools, or juggling two jobs. What consumes children—coloring and playing house? Lucky ducks. It's this kind of headspace that makes it easy for Spirit to speak with them. They also don't have a filter on what adults consider right, wrong, inappropriate, or strange. Think of how they say whatever's on their minds; every day is an episode of *Kids Say the Darndest Things*. Nobody's told them it's weird or crazy to talk about angels, Spirit, or memories from a past life, so sometimes they do. It's us grown-ups who close ourselves off to the unknown in such a quick and judgmental way.

When a child says, "I see dead people," and he or she isn't quoting from the Bruce Willis movie, hear the kid out. Ditto if the child claims to see a monster, shadow, imaginary friend, or ghost. If they say they're seeing Spirit or a loved one who's passed, the best advice is to be open to what they have to say. Don't make a big deal about it, and ask your questions with subtlety. Don't cross-examine the poor dears, but let *them* tell *you* what's going on. You want to make sure that what the child's seeing is real, so you don't want to lead them on at all. In my family, nobody made a fuss about me talking to Spirit, and that implied support was invaluable. Another big point is to pay attention to your child's level of fear. Always let sensitive kids know that there's nothing to be afraid of, and if they're scared, make it clear that they have the power to tell Spirit to leave.

If all signs point to bona fide Spirit and your child is okay with their presence, you can casually say something like, "How nice! Grandpa is watching over you. He's in Heaven now." Showing the child a picture might help confirm that it is, in fact, Grandpa or someone else in your family. If children are too young to process what is happening or if they're too frightened, it's also possible to "shut down" their abilities. You can do this through a healer that you trust or even a therapist who specializes in working with kids who are intuitive. These children's gifts will likely show up again during puberty, and then they can decide whether to develop them further, or if they never want to.

During a recent three-thousand-person reading at a theater in Charlotte, North Carolina, I was instantly drawn to a ten-year-old girl. I could cry right now, remembering this story. She'd lost her sister, who was eight years older, and her sister's soul came through to tell me that she appears to her. The girl was shy when I asked her if this was true. "You're not crazy," I told her. "You have a special, beautiful gift from God. You should enjoy it and embrace it. Receive messages from your sister. She wants you to know she's okay." Her mom then broke down and said they had her in therapy and even installed surveillance cameras in the house because she was so afraid that she was being watched. If her parents didn't trust what their daughter saw, and bring her to experiences like mine, you could see how this poor girl could have been diagnosed with a mental illness like schizophrenia, or something similar. Her sister's soul also told me she was doing something special for Christmas, and Mom said they were thinking of coming to New York. They did, and while she was there, I arranged for her to do a healing with Pat, who taught her protection, grounding, and never to fear what she sees or hears.

Since I feel that my gift is genetic, it's no surprise that young kids in my family tend to sense Spirit. When Victoria was about eight years old, she told me that she didn't want to go in her bedroom alone, much less sleep in there. One night, I fell asleep with her in her bed, but I was quickly woken up by someone poking and pulling the covers off me. It was a little boy's soul, teasing and taunting me, but we didn't have to worry—I then saw my Nanny chasing after him with a pot and telling him to leave us alone! Also, my nephew and godchild Nicholas, Lisa's son, lived in Nanny and Pop's house right after Pop died. As I've said, Lisa is very spiritual and always shared her own Spirit stories with me as a kid. Shortly after Pop passed, Nick was playing in what used to be my grandfather's office and said, "There's a mean man in glasses who yelled at me and told me to get out!" When he said that, I had a flash of what Pop's room used to look like—his messy desk, a leather recliner. We all knew the soul was Pop's. He was very private.

My brother Mike's son Jason, when he was three years old, also saw his grandfather—but on his mom Corrinda's side. Jason had never seen Grandpa Lou or even a picture of him, since he died before Jason was born. One day, Jason told my brother that there was a man in the kitchen with Mommy. Mike came in to see and only found Corrinda. Jason kept pointing and saying, "There he is!" but neither Corrinda nor Mike could see Grandpa Lou. When Corrinda asked what he looked like, Jason described the man as having black hair, and when they showed him a picture of a random person with black hair, Jason shook his head and said, "No, that's not him." So Corrinda went digging for a picture of her dad and when she showed Jason *that* photo, his face dropped. "That's the man," he said. "That's the man who was calling my name." This was the only time Jason experienced this. Of course, Mike called me and said, "Jason's seeing dead people in the pantry, and it's your fault"—and hung up! I suggested they explain who Grandpa Lou was, that he died and was in Heaven, and Jason never saw him or another Spirit again.

But now, a few years later, Corrinda and Mike's eight-year-old daughter Halle began seeing and sensing Spirit—and guess who's back? I recently got this long and baffled text from Corrinda:

Halle is seeing my dad in the middle of the night and constantly waking us up at 3 AM. This morning, she told me that she opened her eyes and saw him standing in her room looking at her. She said she was freaked out and when she got up to come in my room, she walked right through him! I asked her if he said anything and she said no. She said she feels her feet being tickled sometimes, too. I need her to sleep through the night; we are exhausted! Should I sage the house or tell Spirit to go away? Mike and I have also been smelling smoke in our room. I almost went back to Sleepy's for a third time to tell them my mattress was used by a smoker, but it doesn't always smell. My dad was a smoker for many years . . .

Halle is clearly very sensitive to Spirit, so I suggested that Corrinda burn white sage to cleanse the house of Spirit every few weeks. (I personally do this every time a client leaves my home. My husband, Larry, calls sage "Spirit bug spray.") Corrinda now does this, and at night, she also prays that Spirit does not touch, make sounds, or present themselves to her children, and asks them to go to the light. Although Halle still doesn't sleep too well, she hasn't mentioned seeing her grandfather again. I think it helps that she says a little speech of her own before bed, where she says good night to Grandpa Lou, Gram, and all their friends, and asks them to please not touch her, make any noises that could scare her, and to protect her from outside of her room. As for the smoky odor, Corrinda says it did go away for a while, but they still occasionally smell it.

Speaking of Saging . . .

Native Americans have burned dried white sage for purification and protection for centuries, and one thing it helps do is clear any negativity from your house. I know you're not channeling negative Spirit, but just to keep any Spirit activity in your home in a good place, I recommend burning white sage—also called "smudging"— every few weeks. To do this, light a piece or two of dried sage in a shallow ceramic bowl, and then gently blow the flame out until it smokes. Push the smoke up to the ceiling with a feather or fan. Start by facing the front door, and go to your right, following the ceiling all the way around the house to include closets, attics, basements, and garages if they're attached to the house. Pay attention to dark spaces, like the oil burner room, and you can also push some smoke under the bed and on top of it if anyone has trouble sleeping. Do all of this while repeating, "Only Spirits who walk in the white light of God are welcome here. All negative energies must leave by the power of God." I also like to throw out a few positive affirmations and ask that only peaceful feelings, emotions, and thoughts dwell in our home. Let the sage burn until it goes out by itself, and if it dies before you're finished, light another piece and keep going! Keep a window slightly cracked on each floor.

Me? I've Got Spirit Coming Out of My Ears

Although *you* may need to open your awareness to Spirit to experience it, I'm good over here. Your loved ones aren't waiting for you at my house, though they may show up early if I'm meeting with you the next day or that week. Even still, Spirit is always around me. I'm constantly getting messages from my own loved ones who've crossed and those for people I know. I've noticed too that since my life and business have become more public, I'm seeing more Spirit than I ever have before.

It doesn't bother me to hear from the dead so much. I don't constantly listen to them chattering, whispering, laughing, or clomping up and down the stairs. My lights don't flicker all day like I live in a disco. Spirit knows when I'm working, or about to work, and they know when to give me space. Other times, I'll catch a glimpse of energy or feel a presence, and I can decide whether to stay on it or let it pass. It's like being in a crowded city, where people walk right past you, and you don't pay much attention to them after a while—but you can always say hi or stop them to ask for directions, if you want. One time, though, I did see a man peeking in my kitchen window, which really scared me since I usually see Spirit as mists and silhouettes. I knew it wasn't a human person, but he sure looked like one. He was wearing a flannel shirt and looked like the Brawny paper towel guy. I told my first client about him, and she said he fit the description of her brother who had passed. I was like, "Well, your brother just freaked me out, peeping in my window like that!"

Because Spirit's always around me, hoping I'll deliver a message to you, their urgency can happen when it's pretty inconvenient. The first time I ever got my eyebrows waxed at Nordstrom, I had it done by a woman named Geeta, who's since become a friend. As she put hot, sticky wax on my face, I began feeling Spirit all around me. In my head, I was like, *Stay away, Spirit. This is not a good time. I have wax near my eyeballs. I'm not answering you right now*—but the energy was insistent. So I told Spirit that if they really needed me to deliver a message, to put the opportunity in my path. Just then, Geeta spun my chair around, looked at me with wax about to drip off her wooden stick, and said, "Some people say I'm psychic." Geeta didn't know I was a medium, and this was a good four years before the show was on, so I took it as the sign I'd asked for. Apparently, her mother, father, brother, and husband had all died—the woman's in her forties, by the way—and they *all* had messages for her. After getting to know me, she began to develop her intuition and turned it into a gift of healing. She's now a Reiki Master.

Since Spirit's around me so much, I'm not gonna lie—a few times I've used it to my advantage. Oh, come on, wouldn't you? As a mom, being a medium always worked well with keeping my kids in line. I never really knew what was going on with them, but

I'd tell them that I'd send my guides with them when they went out so they'd stay out of trouble! Victoria and my son, Larry, never thought about doing anything bad because they probably thought Spirit would rat them out. I even called them up a few times to find out if they were okay, and said my Spirit guides told me to. But I was just being a nervous mom—Spirit hadn't told me anything! Now that they're older, I don't do this. I don't even think Spirit would help me spy on Victoria at school, or on my son when he's at a bar with his friends. Spirit probably thinks there's a lot that I'm better off not knowing.

I've also asked my angels to help me find a parking spot at the mall or items I've lost around the house. I spend most of my day searching for stuff I've misplaced because I'm such a space cadet, so if I didn't ask for Spirit's help with this, I'd get nothing done. To enlist their aid, I calmly sit down, relax, and pray to St. Anthony, the patron saint of lost articles, that he guide me to where I put the item. You can try this, too. My husband, Larry, always says I can talk to souls across many dimensions, but I can't find the keys in my own damn pocketbook. If I ask for something too silly, my guides don't pay attention. But once I ordered this amazing hand sanitizer for when I was on the road; since I shake so many hands, I don't want to get sick out there. It smelled so good—like lavender, chamomile, eucalyptus, and sage—that I couldn't wait to get it! I'd placed the order a few months back, and the company said it arrived, but I didn't remember seeing the box. So I asked Spirit to guide me to it, and they showed me my husband's business checks. I remembered putting a long, skinny box on his desk that I thought was full of deposit slips, but when I went back to actually open the box, my hand sanitizer was in it!

I'm also frequently asked if I've used my abilities for gambling or the lottery. Get your minds out of the gutter. What I do is for the highest good of all concerned, so I'd never do that intentionally! And let's face it, even if I did try, I'm way too scattered to recognize what I'm being told. My aunt and I went to Belmont Park Race Track for her birthday one year, and I remember hearing "six ten" when I walked in—which is my birthday, June 10. *How nice,* I thought. *Spirit's acknowledging my birthday too.* My uncle asked me what colors I liked best so he could bet on a horse wearing that color, and all the colors I said were losing. It wasn't until after we left that I realized all the horses that won were a combination of the numbers six and ten! And then there was the time I went to a spa with my sister-in-law Corrinda. We went to Mohegan Sun one night, which was the first time I'd ever been to a casino, and decided to play roulette. Wouldn't you know, every number we played on the wheel was a loser?

To me, the best part about opening yourself up to hearing from Spirit is that you can do it just by being yourself. You don't need tarot cards or crystals. You don't even need to hold or wear an object with your family member's energy, like a lot of people think. When I mention a necklace or ring during a session that you've brought with you, it's not because I'm drawn to that energy like a magnet. It's because Spirit tells me to reference it. In fact, I once did a phone reading for a woman who had a lot of female energy around her that had passed on, including a mom, grandmother, aunt, and cousin. She also had a grandfather and father on the Other Side. Anyway, Spirit showed me a picture I have of Victoria, wearing the most random clothes—a baseball cap, sunglasses, Rug Rat pajamas, holding the pet parakeet that Gram got her, and

Mardi Gras beads. So I said, "This is going to sound bizarre, but I feel like you're wearing a strange mix of items: pajamas, a silk scarf, a man's hat, gloves, rosary beads, and jewelry that doesn't match. Are you wearing an article from every dead person you want to hear from?" There was total silence on the phone. "I am," she whispered. I think she was a little embarrassed, but I have to admit that I was actually relieved she didn't dress like that all the time!

Once You're Dead,
Then What?

If you're one of those really busy or active people whose coffee mug says, "I'll rest when I'm dead," I've got news for you—the afterlife is not one long nap. You may rest for a bit, but you've got places to go, Spirit to see. You'll glide around with the amazing ease and serenity that characterizes the Other Side, and not too long after your soul leaves the physical world, Spirit says you'll account for your actions and either stick around Heaven a little longer or prepare to reincarnate with most of your loved ones. I know our souls also have fun, because Spirit loves to laugh. But your soul also has stuff to take care of while it's in Heaven. It doesn't just float around at one big after-party in the sky.

Spirit isn't too detailed with me about what happens after we die, mostly because I've told them that I don't need a play-by-play; I believe there are things we know at a soul level that we aren't intended to realize as humans. I also don't deliberately travel outside my body to other places, and I've never had a near-death experience, so I haven't been to the Other Side to report back. (I have met Gram there in a past-life regression, but there was nothing around us but a white haze; it felt very peaceful, and as much as I love my life here, I didn't want to leave.) But Spirit has shared some cool nuances with me, and I've also picked up on some interesting details while channeling clients' dead friends and family. For me, this is plenty, and I hope it does the trick for you too. It's hard to live fully in this life if you're always thinking about what comes next!

Sweet Surrender

I breezed through what happens when you die in chapter three, but I want to flesh it out a little more here. So when you pass away, Spirit says that the soul lifts out through either your body or head. I'm told that you then enter a tunnel, which you probably already know, since people who've had near-death experiences (NDEs) validate this remarkable journey for us. Better them than me! I'll never ask Spirit to bring me through a tunnel to experience Heaven, not even for this book. Some NDE survivors go on to say that they became aware of nurturing thoughts that reached out to them while floating through a haze that felt like another dimension. This is actually how I feel when I channel, so maybe part of me is on the Other Side during a session, and I just don't know it.

Once you're free of your body, any suffering or ailment you may have felt in the physical world is immediately gone. No matter how tragic, painful, or long-suffering your death, I want to be clear that your soul detaches quickly and peacefully. The souls of people in wheelchairs have shown me they can dance in Heaven, and if a woman died from breast cancer and had a breast removed while she was here, Spirit makes me feel like her soul is full in the chest. Because we don't have bodies in Heaven, I don't think we literally have legs or ample boobs—it's just Spirit's way of saying that pain stays with the physical body and souls move freely on the Other Side. Your soul may feel momentarily sad about leaving loved ones, but you're not overwhelmed with grief the way people in this world are, because your soul quickly becomes aware that you will see them again.

When you enter the afterlife, you're greeted by the joyful souls of family and friends who passed before you and influenced your time here. During a reading, when Spirit shows me a person at the end of a bed with one arm extended, that's my sign for a soul who greeted him or her at the time of death. I can't tell you the number of instances a client has said to me, "That's so crazy, because Mom called her brother's name just before she passed," or "She was reaching to someone we couldn't see as she died." You are guided toward a bright light that is God, no matter what your religion is. Jews don't head to one cloud and Protestants to another. Some NDE survivors also say that they felt guided by musical sounds—not a song per se, but chords, hums, and vibrations. You'll reunite with your primary guide, who's helped you on your spiritual path in this life.

Lights, Camera, Action: This Is Your Life!

Spirit says that the main reason we're here to begin with is to learn certain lessons, and as we do, our soul grows and graduates to different levels of knowledge. This is why, once you're in Heaven, you and your primary guide will review your life on earth. You'll go over everything you did—the good and bad—and evaluate how well you stuck to the path your soul chose and the lessons you were meant to learn during your time here. The review includes experiencing life through the eyes of people you knew in the physical world—you'll feel their pain, happiness, fear, you name it—and you'll understand the chain reactions of your words and behavior. Spirit says this happens pretty quickly and compares it to watching a filmstrip. Though our brains can hardly remember when we walked the dog or sent an important email in the physical world, in Heaven you don't have to worry about recalling anything from your life, because you'll emotionally relive it. As this happens, you'll discuss how you could have spent your time here differently, so certain people wouldn't have experienced negative feelings you inflicted on them. In our world, people who aren't self-aware can be so naïve about how their actions affect others, but in Heaven, you have a clear understanding of all the dynamics.

Though you're held accountable for your actions, and you're evaluated based on how well you understood and executed your role in this life, you aren't chastised for things you did wrong. Cruel punishment and judgment that make you feel bad about yourself are things that we inflict on each other in the physical world. When it comes to being held accountable in Heaven for your past deeds, I'm told that God isn't the fire-and-brimstone figure that some people think. He and your guides are compassionate, and they have unconditional love. They may be disappointed, but from what Spirit shows me, I don't feel there's eternal damnation waiting for the average, flawed person.

I've had souls step forward to apologize or take responsibility for actions, and it's clear that the soul's been through a life review. A client might say, "My father never took ownership for anything!" But in Heaven, souls must. The time it takes for a soul to reach this awareness may explain why it might apologize or discuss a wrong-doing during one reading but not another—at the time, it may not have grown to that level of understanding. Once I read for a young girl whose father left her family many times when she was young. He had no contact with them, sent no money, and acted like they never existed. Eventually, the man remarried and had other kids. When I channeled his departed soul, he said to tell his daughter, "I left because I didn't know how to unconditionally love at that time. I'm not asking for your forgiveness, but I do need you to know how much I love you. Now that my soul has had to relive what it was like for you not to have the father you deserved and needed me to be, I understand, and I am sorry." He went on to explain that he didn't say this so that the girl would forgive him, but so she'd know he was remorseful and being held accountable for his actions. I've even had souls come through and say that if they could do it all over, they'd change certain undesirable characteristics about themselves. When a soul can finally appreciate the upsetting things it did to those in the physical world, with the help of a life review, it not only heals and grows, but it can begin to comfort the people it left behind.

Of course, not every message linked to lessons learned from a life review is heavy. I once channeled a woman's mom who was the first one to step forward during a good-sized group reading. The soul was so proud and said, "I pushed through all those other souls to be heard!" This surprised the daughter, since she said her mom was always the politest wallflower. Looks like she's learning how to be assertive in Heaven!

God's Lesson Plans

I'm under the impression that you have one main lesson to learn in each lifetime, with many smaller teachings tucked into that journey. They include compassion, patience, friendship, selflessness, joy, peace, kindness, goodness, faithfulness, self-control, and unconditional love. For each lifetime you experience, you choose, and then review with God and your primary guide, what you hope to accomplish and what challenges you'll run into as you go. You also choose your family and body, both of which can be related to your lesson. You do this knowing it'll help you get to a new level of spiritual growth.

After your life review, you continue to learn lessons on the Other Side, and at some point, you can do one of two things. Your first option is to stay in Heaven and learn lessons for a while, where teacher-like souls monitor your progress. One reason a soul might choose to hang back is if a previous lifetime felt too hard, and it isn't ready or anxious to return right away. The alternative is to choose a body and return to this world to learn your new lessons at a faster rate, which advances your soul more quickly than if you do this in Heaven. It's like in college, when you can opt to travel abroad or do an internship for a semester versus taking classes; the "real world" experience teaches you things you could never learn in a classroom. Your soul can appreciate fresh perspectives by experiencing different religions, ethnicities, jobs, and family dynamics that cause you to gain greater appreciation and compassion for others. The good news is, I don't think there's a ticking clock that limits the time you have to learn your lessons—you can come back as many times as you need to try again.

The main way you learn lessons in this world is through events that force you to use the traits you're meant to acquire. For example, having a certain disease might teach you about priorities, being in a challenging marriage may require patience and self-reflection, or being bullied as a child could help you learn sympathy toward others. I believe people are placed in our lives to help us to grow and learn as well. Your lessons and purpose may also relate to advancing society in some way—say, through humanitarian, artistic, or scientific efforts. Or it may have to do with a spiritual mission related to self-sacrifice or spreading ideas. No matter what, we're all here to learn how to be better people, and souls, for others. Just as we need their divine guidance, inspiration, and intervention, Spirit needs our capable and eager bodies to act on their behalf.

Since we choose our bodies and the lessons that come with living that life, those with crippling imperfections—a physical handicap, maybe, or a psychiatric struggle related to depression or OCD—have done so to grow their souls in some way. I wish my body were a lot of things it's not—relaxed instead of anxious, five foot seven and a hundred twenty pounds instead of five foot one and . . . never mind. But this package has helped me learn to be grateful and make the most of what I've been given, and it's taught me self-control around my mom's delicious Mickey Mouse–shaped pancakes. I hope it doesn't sound like I'm diminishing serious conditions that people struggle with. I've read for a number of families with kids who are paralyzed, or died from a disease at a young age, and they've all said to me, "No child would *choose* to come here under those circumstances, Theresa." But they do, and you do—your lesson just might not be clear until you're in Heaven. You choose to return to this life when you are in your soul state, so the choice is made not as an emotional human, but as a soul wanting to move closer to God. Also, because your soul chooses your journey for a reason, I smile when people who feel they've been dealt a bad hand ask, "Why would God do this to me?" Neither God nor your soul chose your lesson with naïveté or vindictiveness—again, it's all part of your lesson. On the Other Side, there's no meanness, resentment, or fury. There's only love, because that's what God is.

I know what you're thinking—so what happens to free will? Based on what Spirit says, I believe that the predetermined things in your life that help you learn your lessons are set, and you fill in the rest with your choices. You'd think that fated turns might include taking a first job, meeting your spouse, having a child, or other things you'd consider a milestone here—but they don't have to be. If running your first company isn't part of the lesson you were meant to learn, then it is simply a choice. Similarly, people always ask me who they're destined to marry. Spirit may tell me it's in the cards for you to get married, but they rarely say who you're going to be with, or at least that's not what Spirit does with me. I also think you can choose *not* to make certain decisions, even if they're tied to a lesson, but they'll send you down a new path, and you'll have to learn your lessons in other ways. (Your "instincts" may let you know if you're about to make a funky turn. What we consider the path of least resistance may simply be, in spiritual terms, the better path.) But if everything were predetermined, there'd be no point to coming here, since your lessons often come from the decisions you make. So you can't change your destiny, but you can tweak how you get there. The good news is that God, your guides, angels, and loved ones will always help you, if you choose to let them. If you don't ask for help, they will not interfere with your freewill choice.

God has given you free will to make your life your own, but when you're on a good path, you'll know it in your soul. When I became an adult, I filled my life with a lot of love and laughter—I married a wonderful man, had beautiful kids, spent time with friends and family, and got a good job that paid the bills. These are all the things you think, and are told, will fulfill you. And don't get me wrong, they mean a lot. But it wasn't until I accepted my gift that my soul felt complete. I was finally on the right path. God had given me the canvas, but it was up to me to paint a beautiful picture, and there was something missing in the landscape until I did the work that satisfied my soul. It's like I'd painted the trees, hills, and sky, but left out the focal point. God's given you a canvas too, and like me, you need to find what makes your picture a masterpiece.

Now, to make sure you don't spin *entirely* off course and paint an ugly baboon in the middle of a scenic French countryside, Spirit's told me that your guides show you predetermined "road signs" throughout your life. These are meant to steer you in a new direction, one that's connected to a lesson or person you're meant to meet. For example, you may see a person wearing a sparkly necklace, notice the way a stranger touches his hair, smell a sharp fragrance—and in your soul's memory, a flag will go up to remind you that you're meant to know each other and learn a significant lesson. Your souls will recognize and be drawn to each other on a deep level.

For everyday choices, your deceased loved ones can also intervene, especially when you notice that someone's put in your path for a reason. This comes up a lot when people start dating after losing their spouses. I once read a woman whose mother came through and said, "I placed that man in your path for you to love"—and when I passed this on, the woman said, "Oh my God, I knew it was my mom!" I also know a man who began dating six months after his wife died from a painful brain tumor. His friends and family were upset, but the woman fit into his life so easily that it had to be kismet. She too had lost her spouse around the same time, they lived in the same community, they both loved to play golf, and they even had vacation homes on the same island without knowing it. I would bet money that the man's deceased wife played matchmaker from Heaven. Souls don't get jealous—they want you to move on in a healthy way.

I'll bet all you overachieving readers are wondering if it's possible to identify your lesson or purpose now, so you can make the most of your time here. In the school of life, you want to take extra classes so you can graduate with honors? Okay, sure, you can try to do that. It is called soul searching, and you can do it through guided meditation. You may even get some help from Spirit. You can also soul search during yoga, prayer, or anytime you have focused intentions or a clear and relaxed mind. Think about what makes you happy, what you can do better, and what you've done to make others happy, and your lesson might bubble up. And while you've got Spirit's attention, you should also think about how the people in your life relate to your lesson. You may think of them in a whole new light and decide to approach them in a way that benefits your souls.

Going Up?

Spirit shows me that you enter the afterlife at a certain "level," or point of spiritual growth, and that your life assessment is based on that level's criteria. Think of a level like a grade in school—the lower it is, the more lessons the soul has to learn. As a soul advances, it moves up to new levels. It happens gradually, and you must complete one level before moving higher or deeper into the next. I don't know how many levels there are on the Other Side, but if I'm correctly interpreting what Spirit's told me, I believe there are also many levels within a dimension. So if you've finished a series of lessons in one dimension, you can move to a new dimension where there are new lessons to learn. You can also ascend in Heaven to become a guide, teacher, or hold another title (I'm sure there are more responsibilities than I know about). It sounds similar to how we earn different degrees in this world—from a basic high school diploma to more advanced degrees and letters after our names—to help prepare us for different types of jobs.

Levels aren't just "grades" of learning; they also refer to the energy's frequency. So when a soul grows, it also raises its level or wavelength. On the lowest level of the Other Side are the souls of people who learned very few lessons and did real damage in our world, like some criminals and abusers. They won't stay on this level forever, and they have a lot of learning to do over there; but eventually, they'll grow their souls and raise their levels. At the highest level of Heaven is God. When I channel, I enter at a higher (but realistic) level and have all the souls meet me there. Spirit can come down a level, but it can't go up unless it's earned this. For instance, I once read a woman who'd lost both of her parents. Mom was amazing, but dad was an alcoholic, abusive pain in the tush. Mom's soul brought the father's soul forward, but she had to lower her vibration to do it because they were at different levels.

You've probably noticed that I use the terms "Heaven" and "The Other Side" interchangeably, and I think Spirit lets me do this so that I am comfortable meshing my faith with other aspects of the spiritual world. To me, Heaven *is* the Other Side and nearly all of us go there. I also think of the afterlife this way because I believe that God is in Heaven, and He is the source of unconditional love, overwhelming peace, brilliant light, and all of creation. But because there's good in the universe, I know there also has to be bad, so if I say there's a Heaven, you'd assume there must also be a Hell. This is where my own interpretations of the Other Side come in, based on what Spirit has shown me and what I've experienced during readings. Take it for what you wish!

Though Spirit might reference low levels on the Other Side when I channel, they've never used the word "Hell" with me. This may be a place where pure evil resides, or may be how lower levels were interpreted in the Bible, because like I said, low levels are where troubled souls enter the afterlife, so these parallels could make sense. The term "*under*world" even is often used interchangeably with "Hell," which also fits into what Spirit tells me because if you think of "Hell" relative to the more righteous, higher levels *above* it, I could see how people would say Hell is under Heaven, because low levels are under higher ones. If Hell is anything more than this, then I'm not sure what or who is there, because I don't deal with negative Spirits like poltergeists, and I only read lower-level souls if higher-level souls bring them forward. Regardless, I want you to know that souls that enter at low levels do not get a free ride, and their like-minded company isn't much fun to hang out with, to say the least. These souls have to put in their time and work to do better. They also keep at it on the Other Side or by reincarnating, until they get their lessons right, since I can't imagine that most souls would want to be at a level filled with other, lesser souls for eternity. People don't want to live in bad neighborhoods here, and I'll bet it's the same for souls in the afterlife. But I believe you can do your learning with a peaceful spirit and with a loving, forgiving God. This isn't my religious belief; it's just what Spirit's told me. Why should a soul have to learn lessons in a torturous place?

This isn't easy for everyone to hear. A few years ago, I channeled a girl who was murdered by her best friend's ex-boyfriend. He killed her and then killed himself. The mom, dad, and two brothers were all there. When the girl's soul came through, she said, "Theresa, my brothers aren't going to like this, but I'm going to bring forward the soul of the boy who killed me." So she did, and he apologized to her mom for his crime. The man's soul said, "I am sorry for taking your most precious gift." The brothers were freaking-out furious about this. "Why is she with him?" they wanted to know. But she wasn't *with* him. She lowered her vibration to his level to bring the soul forward and give her mom healing. Not only was the mother grieving her daughter's death, but she'd made herself sick wondering if the man felt remorse for what he did. His soul went on to say that not only does it have to account for his grave deed, but he must endure the family's heartache over the life he took. The message also validated that the girl's soul hears her mom's thoughts. She didn't bring the guy's soul forward for the fun of it.

As a medium, I've discovered more than I ever thought I'd know about life and death. But struggling clients like this family, and truly remorseful souls, have taught me so much about forgiveness and how essential it is to heal our pain. I used to be a very cut-and-dried person—if you did something to me, I was done with you. But I've gotten better. I think it's hard to dig deep, figure out what's wrong, and fix it. But that's what our souls, and the people in our life, need us to do. Learning forgiveness is like taking out the trash. If you don't deal with it right away, the garbage will pile up, begin to smell like chocolate-covered onions, and you'll have to do an even bigger cleanup later.

When It's Your Time, It's Your Time

Spirit says that the time you're destined to die is generally set, but how we reach that point is up to the choices we make. I've never heard of there being a specific date that you're due to check out; it's more like a window of time. Is it years, weeks, days? I don't know. But when you hear about freak accidents, or unfair twists of fate, like a guy who misses his flight, the plane crashes without him on it, and a week later he dies in a car accident—that's what I'm talking about here. And remember that story about journalist Jessica Ghawi, who escaped death by a gunman in a Toronto mall and blogged, "I was reminded that we don't know when or where our time on Earth will end. When or where we'll take our last breath"? A month later in Aurora, Colorado, she was shot during that horrible, horrible midnight screening of the Batman film *The Dark Knight Rises.* Hello, destiny. On the flip side, there's truth to the old saying "It wasn't his time to go," which is what I thought about when I met a man who'd tried to commit suicide by throwing himself out a window but lived fifteen more years in a wheelchair.

I guess Spirit isn't more specific about how we'll pass because we do have free will, but that's yet another reason to live each day in a way that we want to be remembered. I recall channeling a young boy who died in Florida while horsing around with his friends in a car. He was in one vehicle and he mooned his friends in another; when he lost his balance, he fell into the driver, who crashed the car. Though the kid who was joking around died, mooning was not specifically written into his life plan. God wasn't like, *Okay, so here's how it all ends. You're going to pull down your pants, cause a lot of commotion, and then your life's kaput.* I believe the boy was destined to die within a certain block of time, and he made a choice that determined mooning would be his exit.

I do, however, think that our souls may know when we're close to death, and the memo can slip through the conscious mind. My cousin Al suffered from liver disease, and while he was undergoing treatment, I ran into him at a party. He told me the doctors gave him a clean bill of health, but I sensed otherwise. A few days later, he showed up at my house unannounced to fix my toilet, although I'd been bugging him about this for weeks. Two days later, he died. I felt like his soul was tying up loose ends, and that included my plumbing. I also know a woman whose father took care of his sick wife for many difficult years. One night, the dad called his daughter up and said, "Can you please come over and sit with your mom? She's in a lot of pain." The woman was making dinner for her kids and preparing for a meeting at work the next day. She always rushed to her parents' side, but for the first time in years, asked for a pass. "I'll come by tomorrow and call in twenty minutes." When she did, her dad said Mom was better, but before hanging up, he added, "Do you think there's a place for me in

Heaven?" "Of course," she said. "Don't talk like that." That night, her father died in his sleep. I believe his soul knew that it would soon be leaving this world, even if his brain didn't.

Now, if our destiny is set, does that leave room for miracles? Absolutely! But I actually think miracles just change the way we reach our destiny; they don't change the ending itself. So while we usually think of a miracle as something outside of what is meant to happen, I think that the miracle is part of your journey. Spirit tells me that rarely do miracles happen and then the people who experienced them go back to a hum-da-dum life. They usually teach others what they've learned, or pay it forward, and try to do or be more than before. So God knows that at some point in your time here, you'll survive the impossible—a drowning, a fire, a terminal medical diagnosis—and people will call it a miracle, but it was really part of a bigger plan for you to talk about it, write about it, change lives, and spread the word about what you've learned.

As a medium whose job involves meeting a lot of devastated people, I've found that when there's a sudden death, like a car accident, families and friends connected to those who passed are so shocked, confused, and heartbroken that they don't know where to funnel their energy, so they look for a person to blame. When this happens, Spirit always urges me to talk about how we make choices in the physical world that lead to the time of a death. During a show in Atlantic City, I read for a girl who lost friends in a car accident—four people died, but four others lived. Later that day, during the very next show, who comes but the family of one of the boys who died. (When I started channeling, I was confused; Spirit's a big fan, but souls rarely attend more than one show at a time!)

In both readings, the same departed souls stepped forward to talk about how much finger-pointing was going on between the families of those who survived and those who didn't. The overwhelming message from the dead was: "Stop blaming the survivors. We all made choices that day." The car wasn't made to fit eight people, so every person in the accident decided to pile in. The souls also kept showing me the passengers switching seats, and those who lived had survivor's guilt. The destiny theme also couldn't be clearer—that some died that day and others lived, yet all made choices that led to their fates.

I really love how Spirit brought all these families together so they could hear messages that could help their anger and sadness. Actually, a similar thing happened during a show in San Diego. I learned that a boy crashed his car while driving next to his girlfriend in her car. The boy died, but the girl lived. A friend of the boy's mom was at the event, sitting orchestra center, and his soul told me to say that his mom was still so angry and blamed the girlfriend for causing the crash. But the soul said, "It wasn't her fault. It was an accident." Suddenly, another woman stood up in balcony house right. "It *was* an accident," she echoed. "He's talking about my daughter. She didn't do anything wrong." It was the girlfriend's mom! She projected so clearly and loudly that she didn't need a mic! What are the odds? Pretty good, I guess, when Spirit wants to make a point.

This Ain't Your First Rodeo

Though you can't fully remember them in your conscious mind, Spirit tells me you've had many lives before this one. Once you're in Heaven, if your soul decides to reincarnate, it will choose where, when, and who it wants to be in the physical world, for the purpose of learning another lesson and helping others. Again, we reincarnate so our soul can grow in a way that aligns with God's; understanding, appreciating, and experiencing different types of lives can help us achieve spiritual balance.

One way to learn about your previous lives is through a regression that's done through hypnosis. This method helps relax the conscious mind and allows access to the memories of your previous experiences in the physical world. Just as your life now is full of positive and negative decisions that impact your health and psyche, so were your prior choices, and these memories are ingrained in your soul. Some people do regressions because they're curious about who they've been in earlier lifetimes and want to meet their guides and angels, which can be done this way. Others explore past lives to find out why they repeat certain habits or to help them understand and heal chronic fears and phobias. Once you recognize old patterning during a regression, it helps resolve that issue in your present life.

Current relationship issues are also seen, understood, and released. I remember one reading I did with a client who told me she obsessively watched over her daughter when she was near water, especially their pool. Spirit told me that in a previous life, the woman lost her eleven-year-old child to a drowning, and her child in this life was approaching that age. That's why her soul was becoming increasingly worried—it remembered the incident. I suggested she revisit her past life with a hypnotist, and when she did, she left all of her fears, emotion, and energy in the past. Pat, who conducts past-life regressions, says you can even have an illness with no obvious cause (chronic pain comes up a lot) that's rooted in things that happened to you in a prior life.

Because of my Catholic upbringing, it took a minute for me to accept that we used to have past lives. I just thought we died, went to Heaven, and that was it. And whenever I heard about regressions from others who'd done them, I wondered why they always sounded almost too dramatic or fascinating to be true. You were Amelia Earhart in a past life? A Trojan warrior, really? But if you think about it, we all have a story. It's funny to consider your life now, or even a friend's, and how it would sound as a past-life regression narrative. *You married a soldier who was the love of your life, but he died young.* Or, *your father was a wealthy businessman but you never knew your mother. You later had three kids, and one passed in a car accident.* Or, *you never had children but married a celebrity and had many loving pets, and this fulfilled you in every way.* Suddenly, it doesn't seem like such a leap of faith, right?

The first time I had Pat do a past-life regression on me was to overcome some phobias, and I was just blown away. I learned that in one life, I was a boy searching for my younger brother in a house fire, and when I looked into his eyes, I saw my daughter, Victoria; she played this role in that lifetime. I think it explains why I feel an overwhelming need to keep tabs on her more than my son. I've also been a princess kidnapped by pirates on a ship, during a wild rainstorm. Here I was held prisoner, raped, and murdered. I believe this contributes to why I was afraid of rain for so many years—because really, who's afraid of rain? And to understand why I don't like enclosed spaces, I was told that I was an Egyptian queen who was buried alive with her husband. I've also been a medicine woman and an Indian chief, which makes sense since I'm inexplicably drawn to Native American culture. This is also interesting to me, because when I look at a photograph of an Indian chief in a full headdress, I can stare into his eyes and feel a kind of familiarity and kinship—as if I'd done the same thing as him at some point.

More recently, I did a regression to shed light on why I'm doing the work I do. We put this on *Long Island Medium,* so it may sound familiar. Pat did the honors, and she brought me back to lifetimes that were very tragic. I learned it's because I overcame these events with the ability to still love unconditionally that I was given the gift I have. In these lives, I was an official during the Roman Empire who was killed on my son's wedding day, a young girl who was held prisoner in a jail for a crime that wasn't her fault, a child with a joyful soul despite a crippling disability, and an orphan in Russia. This last one had a tremendous impact on my soul. After the man who ran the facility took me in, I stayed on to work with him and care for the other children. I overcame my struggles and paid it forward. In this life, the man who ran the orphanage is now my son, Larry, and a child who did not want to leave when he was adopted is my nephew Jason. I believe this moving lifetime is one of the reasons I get along so well with kids, and why the souls of children who've passed say they like channeling through me. If you're interested in knowing about your past life, I say go for it. But before seeing a specialist, be sure to learn more about the topic first to put your expectations in check, and research trustworthy recommendations before choosing a hypnotist.

You can also catch a glimpse of your past lives on your own and without a regression, which is called déjà vu. This is when you remember something your soul did in a previous life. It usually comes as a familiar and seemingly inexplicable feeling: you're in a house, town, neighborhood, or another country that you've never visited before but everything seems familiar. You might not even recognize the aha! moment right away; you just know that you feel calm and settled while you're there.

You can feel déjà vu with people you've never met but who don't seem like total strangers. I've been close to my friend Eileen for twenty-three years, and I'm sure we had other lives together. She stuck by me as I figured out my phobias and gift, with devoted friendship. I've wondered if I was helpful to her in a past life, and if being there for me in this one was part of her lesson, because I trusted Eileen in situations where I wouldn't have trusted many other people, and she understood me in ways that few friends did.

So why don't you naturally remember your past lives, especially if they can teach you so much about yourself? Spirit has said this would hold you back; if you have a foot in each journey, then you won't make the most of your life this time around. This is also the reason you forget what happens in Heaven once you're born—so you can stay in the moment here. And since the spiritual point of life is to learn lessons, I think you also learn better when you start fresh. You're meant to make freewill decisions, and when you're up against temptation, negativity, or unfairness of any kind, your choices would mean much less, and you might not even try as hard, if you remembered how good you have it in Heaven. It's like you need the spiritual amnesia or it would be tough to prioritize what mattered in the past and what you should pay attention to now.

I also think spiritual memory loss is a little like how you don't recall the pain of having a baby. If you did, women would think much harder before growing their families. But if you really think about it, how *do* women forget what the feeling is like? My husband had intense brain surgery to remove a tumor, and he will never forget that pain. How can he recall what it felt like to have his head cut open, but I can't remember what it's like to push a small human out of my body? The answer: because amnesia is part of the procreating process, and it's to your benefit to forget. If you did remember, you might get so focused on all the gory details that you wouldn't be able to lose yourself in the moments that help make babies in the first place, if you know what I mean.

When I was twenty-eight years old, my guides told me that this is my soul's last journey in the physical world. After I die, my soul is going to stay in Heaven. It made me a little sad to hear that I wouldn't be coming back, but I'm not going to worry about it. Maybe I'll be a guide, or do another job that doesn't require a physical body. If it is my last hoorah, I can't complain. This has been a really good life for me.

What Goes Around, Comes Around

I'll be honest: I don't know how much Karma—the laws of cause and effect that are said to dictate our lives—determines our good and bad fortune in our many existences. People who believe in Karma, even casually, think that the way we treat others, the mistakes we make, and the successes that we have will impact both this life and carry into future ones when we reincarnate. If something seems unfair or hard in this incarnation, they say it may be your Karma balancing itself out. Karma is the result of the negative and positive actions we demonstrate; it implies that we can't escape from our past, especially when we harm others, and that everything will catch up to us in this life or future ones.

We like to say that Karma's a bitch, but it also can be a blessing. Karma isn't only about punishment and reward, but yet another way we're supposed to learn lessons, exercise free will in a good way, and have positive behavior reinforced. We have the ability to make corrections and changes in our life when we suspect we're off, and our Karmic patterns adjust accordingly. So if you bring your neighbor soup when he's sick, the good Karma may help you live a long, healthy life; or if you're a selfish wife who never spends time with her family, you may have to care for a sick husband when he's old. Of course, a Karmic payout may not happen in this lifetime. You could hurt your brother tomorrow and learn what it's like to be at his mercy two lives from now. So if you believe in Karma, then we are all here to balance it—to right our wrongs and enjoy the full circle moments of our good deeds. What I'm very sure about is that Karma is not the result of God turning on you. He doesn't punish you for gossiping by giving you cancer. Getting sick may have a reason, but it's not God's vengeance.

I also believe you're here to pay it forward and teach by example, which can lend itself to positive Karma. There's nothing I love more than being on the receiving end of a good deed and then repaying it to others. It reminds me of those news stories about coffeehouse customers who pay for the order of the person in line behind them, and then the next person pays for the guy behind him, and so on, until the trend continues for three hours and hundreds of customers. They always say the best part isn't the "free" coffee, but how good it felt to do something nice for a stranger.

Soul Connections

You know how I said that when you die, you're greeted by Spirit that meant a lot to you in this life? Well, I'm told that for most people, your family and friends wait for you to gather, reunite, and then enter new physical bodies again, if the soul doesn't choose to stay in Heaven. (I have channeled infant and child souls that reincarnated in a parent's lifetime, but that's happened only a few times.) From what Spirit suggests, people in your immediate circle travel the most with you through time, as both relatives and friends, but your relationships to them change, based on what your lesson and soul's purpose is.

I picture life, and the people in it, like an episode of *Saturday Night Live*—and I'm not just saying that because they do an awesome impersonation of me and Larry! On *SNL*, the actors put on different costumes, talk in a bunch of accents, and play a new role in each skit they're in, and those skits make up an entire episode. The cast overlaps in most sketches, but not all of them. This is similar to how the souls of our family and friends reincarnate. Some people call it a soul group, but Spirit's never used that term with me, so I like to call it a soul circle—like a circle of friends, or family circle, that is bonded by a never-ending loop. They're like a cast that plays different roles in each of your lives, and the sum of those lives creates your soul's total experience in the physical world. As on *SNL*, you don't always play the same role in every life or skit—you're not always a mom or wife, for instance. You also do a lot of "costume changes" with races and new bodies (my guides joke that it would be boring to always come back as the same type of person). Because souls don't always choose to reincarnate, you might not be in *every* sketch with the same performers, but they'll join you again before you no longer reincarnate and your episode is over. When we greet each other and reunite in Heaven, it also reminds me of the end of *SNL*, when all the cast members hug each other and laugh. They act so happy to see each other, as if it's been years and years.

People who aren't in your immediate soul circle make cameos in your lives too. Acquaintances can reincarnate with you, but I'm not sure how far-reaching this is. I do know that people in your inner circle don't surface as acquaintances in other lives. So your husband in this life wasn't your butcher in a prior one, but he could be your cousin in the next. A lot of clients who grow their family through an egg donor, sperm donor, or adoption also ask me about soul circles since all or some of a child's DNA can come from a "stranger." But Spirit insists these souls are as much a part of your circle as when they come from your family tree; what matters isn't their genetics but that their souls chose you as their parents and have been connected to you in past lives. You pick your mom and dad before incarnating, and the choice helps you learn or teach a lesson or grow in some way. So if dear old Dad drives you up the frigging wall, how you choose to manage his behavior is likely part of a greater plan or possibly even a Karmic payout. The good news is that you, he, or both of you will benefit from this in the long term.

Soul circles also help explain relationship bonds or tension that you experience in this lifetime. For example, the lingering chemistry you may feel with an ex can make it really confusing when a relationship ends. You might think, *I thought we had a deep connection* . . . Well, guess what? You probably did, but in another life! And if you don't get along with someone, like a boss or in-law, that can also be traced to a previous experience. However, prior lives don't influence *every* nook and cranny of your casual relationships because you do have free will, and you need to take responsibility for your choices and behavior. It's not a good idea to use a past-life excuse to be a creep.

Before we move on, let's talk soul mates for a minute. Most corny books and rom-coms would have you believe that your soul mate is always a romantic or sexual connection, but I don't believe this. I think a soul mate is someone who completes your being and is really easy for you to be around. You feel deeply connected in a visceral way. If we want to keep going on the *SNL* metaphor, I suspect Tina Fey and Amy Poehler are soul mates—they're like two peas in a pod, those two. I once read a woman whose sister died, and her soul had me say, "The day I died, you lost part of your soul." The girl thought it was a little creepy that I basically called her sister a soul mate, but it's very natural. A lot of us feel that our closest soul mate is our spouse or partner, but for plenty of people, it may be another family member or close friend. It could also be a child. It doesn't matter how long the person is with us on earth either. You can tell who your soul mate is by the impact this person has, or had, on you while you were both here. I think my cousin Lisa is a soul I've traveled with through many lifetimes as family or a friend—and absolutely, I'd call her a soul mate. We finish each other's sentences and just when I'm about to pick up the phone to call her, she rings me first. But you know, I don't think I have only one soul mate. I'm not sure if this is typical, but I feel deeply connected to a lot of people in my life, including Larry, Pat, and my mom, so I can't name just one person. And I'm not saying that so they don't kill me!

God and His Humbling Abode

From the time I was young, I believed in God and knew He lived in Heaven. But a little like George and Louise Jefferson, I imagined His home to be a *deluxe* apartment in the sky. It wasn't until I started channeling the deceased, hearing about near-death experiences, and talking to God that I got a very different picture of what it's like there. In the last chapter, I told you what Spirit says you *do* on the Other Side, but here, I want to talk about God, prayer, and all the stuff that contributes to making Heaven such an overwhelmingly magnificent place—how it feels, looks, and even the souls of surprise guests that you might bump into when you get there.

You know by now that I consider myself to be spiritual and have a very strong faith. I don't think you need to be one or the other. Yes, I talk to dead people, but I also pray and go to church every Sunday, and I give as much of my time and money to my parish and other charities as I can. So what does that make me?

Spireligious? I have no idea. Labels aren't my thing, and I'm also under the impression that God's just not that into them either. The last time we talked, He said, bottom line, that as long as people believe and have faith in Him, that's what matters.

I used to reference God only if people asked about Him. I've learned as a medium that clients struggle with religion, particularly after the loss of a loved one, and part of my job is to provide comfort to those who are grieving in a way they can appreciate. You might not want to hear about God, but referring to Him as the source of creation or a powerful energy, and to myself as a "light worker" even, may help take away the intimidation or pressure that can come with organized beliefs. But lately, I've actually found that more clients want to know about God and have questions about Him. I think this has to do with a universal change in perspective going on that some have called an "energy shift." Anyway, I'm always happy to talk about God, because, remember, one reason it took me so long to accept my gift was that I had to figure out how to do this without neglecting my faith. So if more people want to say the G-word, be my guest.

Though I'm not out to convert anyone, and you won't find me thumping on a Bible anytime soon, I like telling stories about feeling God's presence and sharing the messages I get directly from Him. I hope this also helps people trust that my ability comes from a beautiful and divine place. When we first meet, strangers can seem so nervous about seeing a medium or hearing me talk to dead people. *What will my church think? What if she's a witch?* First, holy texts from many faiths recognize spiritual gifts like mine in a positive way—especially if they're used for counseling, healing, teaching, and other moral purposes. Also, there's good and bad in any profession—incredible doctors who save lives, and sloppy ones who commit malpractice; admirable policemen who uphold laws, and corrupt ones who accept bribes. Mediums can play it the same way. Some channel from God, good Spirit, and do wonderful things with the messages they receive, while others get their information from places I don't want to know about. But I'm certain that God is my source, and I trust what the souls who walk in His light tell me.

God 101

Let's start with a few basics about God. First, He is peaceful, supportive, nonjudgmental, and protective. He is the creator of all things and infinite, unconditional love. When you die, you will encounter God, but He's not an old man with a white beard like you see in paintings. God is big energy, similar to how we're also energy before and after we have bodies, but He's way more powerful than we'll ever be (if I surround people, myself, or objects with God's white light in the physical world, I'm essentially surrounding them with a piece of God). Because God isn't a person, I don't think that God is a He, She, or It; but I use masculine pronouns when I talk about God, because it's the most recognizable way to reference Him. Like God, your departed loved ones also don't have a sex—none of our souls do when we are in Heaven—but they present themselves to me with human traits, like gender, so that you can recognize them.

When you cross over, your energy merges with God's, so you

don't so much "meet" God, as "join" or "unite" with Him. On earth, our souls are part of God's, but it is easy to feel disconnected from Him because our bodies and choices can be flawed and challenging. But on the Other Side, your souls are literally part of God. Think of it like a Christmas tree—an ornament can be spectacular on its own (us), but also part of a bigger, more majestic whole (God). Spirit has also shown this relationship to me as one giant, fluffy cloud that separates into many smaller ones.

One God, Many Faiths

As I've said, I feel there is only one God, no matter what your faith is. And though God and religion are typically seen as being intertwined, they really aren't the same thing. God is a positive, pure, and good entity, and religion is a set of beliefs and practices created to serve and worship God. You can use religion to follow God's ways, but I don't feel that God aligns Himself with one faith over another. I love that many religions provide important ethical and spiritual guidance to their communities and encourage charity to those who need it. What I'm not crazy about is how some people think God prefers one religion over another, which, to an extreme degree, has triggered violence, hate, and condemnation between those who claim to be "right" about whose God is The God. It's our egos that cause us to believe our group or values are the only acceptable ones out there, and that's not the case. Bloated self-worth doesn't just shape some religions either; it affects the way we talk about politics, race, and even our favorite sports teams.

Spirit has never told me that God plays favorites, but they *have* said there is one God, and we are all united in Him. During the televised memorial for the devastating massacre in Newtown, Connecticut, I was struck by how many of the world's religions were represented on that stage and thought about how meaningful that must be to God. There were Hebrew chants, references to Jesus, Muslim and Baha'i speakers, and I think I even heard someone refer to God as "Great Spirit." It was an inclusive approach to all faiths, united under one God, and it helped bring people together when they needed each other the most. We may have our differences, but we are all His children.

If the name God is too religious for you to embrace, then Spirit says that Higher Power works for Him too. Personally, I don't care what you call God. Our source of creation is the same entity, no matter what name is attached. If I had to sum up the essence of God and Heaven, I'd say it's about love and how we're all connected to each other in our world and the afterlife. God wants us to rediscover a communal feeling of togetherness with Him to help us feel less alone here.

Are You There, God? It's Me, Theresa!

I feel God around me all the time, but I've only spoken to Him on a few occasions. One of the most moving conversations we had was when I accepted my gift. I was hemming and hawing over whether it was real, and if I could handle the responsibility of channeling souls for those who were grieving. That's when my guides brought out the big guns to assure me that being a medium was what I was called to do. They initiated a conversation with God.

As I channeled the most powerful, calming sensation I'd ever experienced in my life, God basically told me that people were losing faith. They were disappointed with religion, especially those who hid behind it or manipulated its intentions to do immoral or unkind things. Religion was dividing us, rather than bringing us together. He also said that fewer people believed in Him than ever before, and that there needed to be another way to restore faith without preaching, scolding, or knocking on doors. This is where I came in.

God said that I was to reconnect people with their loved ones who died, help them find healing and embrace life, and by proxy, He hoped that they'd come to realize that there's more to life than what's in this one—that is, belief in an afterlife with God. Compared to straight-up dogma or religious proselytizing, he said my channeling would be a newer way to reach people with His messages of love and unity. As I describe this effect to you, Chief shows it to me like an applause meter. Right now, there are fewer people "clapping," which is Chief's metaphor for turning to God. He wants us to be "clapping" more—believing in, talking to, showing gratitude to, and doing good works for Him.

When God told me that people have lost faith in Him, it made me realize how fragile our spiritual beliefs really are. If you have a bad experience with a teacher, you don't immediately lose hope in the whole education system, and if you have a lousy encounter with a doctor, you don't insist that all medical professionals are crap. No, you find teachers and doctors that you can trust, and over time, they show you that you can depend on them. Yet people will turn entirely away from God very easily, if life lets them down. Believe me, I understand why you might get upset with God when you lose family members or life forces you to make hard choices. My heart goes out to you, and in my own ways, I have been there myself. The physical world is tough and you do the best you can to keep your head above water sometimes. But just because a religion, church, leader, or friend lets you down, you can't lose faith in the bigger picture of God and all that He is. Not for nothin', but it's like you're chopping off your nose to spite your face.

So why does God give a rip if you have more faith? Is it for your benefit, or to populate the higher levels of Heaven, or to worship Him more and better? I've gotta tell you, the answer is so simple and yet so challenging at the same time. God basically told me that people don't love and respect each other the way they should, and He'd like us to change that. Not so that He can control us or anything, but so that we can have a better life on earth and get as close to feeling the unconditional love, generosity, and peacefulness of God in our everyday lives as we can. In a nutshell, demonstrating love and compassion will get us back to our most spiritual selves. And I don't want to put words in God's mouth, but I feel like He doesn't want us to have to wait until we're on the Other Side to feel a little piece of Heaven. Our journey here is hard enough without piling on the additional stress and sadness that we inflict on each other every day.

On many occasions, Spirit has told me that we're losing the communal values that keep our souls connected in this world. Small acts like holding the door for others, helping a stranger carry a package, treating people who are different from us as our equals, and checking in on our neighbors can make a huge impact on us and the world in general. God wants us to be generous, kind, grateful, and pay it forward. It's like when you walk into the grocery store, pissed off at your spouse, and as you leave, the bag rips, your oranges go rolling—it's a mess. But then a stranger shows up out of nowhere and helps. He rebags your groceries, holds the door, carries everything to the car, and tells a joke that makes you laugh. Your mood lifts, you go home, and you make peace with your family. All this because one person took ten minutes to make your life a little easier.

In a way, what I think God wants are more angels on earth. He wants to give us one more reason to feel grateful for what we've earned and what He's given to us in the physical world. He wants to make it easier to love and honor ourselves so that we can truly love, honor, and help other people. And wouldn't it be amazing if it became second nature? I hope we're on our way. Think about how many natural disasters we've had in the past few years— destructive blizzards, hurricanes, tornadoes, floods. I don't think God's out to destroy communities so we can pay attention to what matters (we've done a lot of this to ourselves by choosing to wreck the environment), but I do think He's pleased that if something good has to come out of these life-altering events, it's that we're forced to rebuild our communities and the relationships in them.

When God Speaks, Clients Listen

God has also come through for my clients directly—though one time, He made Himself known in a way that I couldn't understand at first. I didn't know anything about the woman I was reading, and she had a quiet demeanor so we didn't really talk much before. One of the first things I said to her was, "There's a husband energy here. Did you lose your spouse?" She told me she never married, so I moved on, but this husband figure wouldn't leave me alone—he even kept showing me a plain, gold wedding band. I passed, and we moved on to other messages, including how she has a spiritual gift like mine. Then during the last fifteen minutes of her reading, I felt a tremendous sense of peace and saw the overwhelming white light with golden edges that always bowls me over.

"Call me crazy, but I feel God is present," I said. I felt different from when I channel a normal husband energy; it felt higher than your loved ones, higher than a guide or angel. God said to tell her, "Thank you for doing my work." The woman thanked me for the reading, and I didn't think about it too much after that. Cut to a few months later, and I was about to read another client when she said, "I heard you gave Sister Mary Catherine the most amazing reading." I was like, *Sister Mary who?* Apparently, the first woman was a *nun*—with psychic abilities, no less—but more than anything, the husband energy now made sense! At first, it didn't feel like God because Spirit makes me feel the bond that the person shares with the soul, but nuns believe they are married to Christ. Plus, He showed me the wedding band. But when we didn't connect with that, God made Himself a lot more obvious! Sheesh, talk about a blond moment on my part.

For as much as God's making the most of my life here, none of it is about me. This is about you and Him. I may have fun with my image—the hair, the nails, the bling—but I am who I am, and all God cares about is that I get His point across. I consider what I do to be God's work, and I know I'm doing it right when I help restore the faith that He's told me has diminished. Consider the time I read a young man who lost his dad, whose soul told me he loved to sing and was very religious when he was in the physical world. The man validated this and then said, "I used to sing too. But the day my dad died, I stopped." During the reading, Dad's soul said he was so proud of his son for following in his footsteps by joining the army. I sensed that the man's heart softened with every word. As we said good-bye, I thought, *If this kid suddenly belts out "Jesus Loves Me," I'll poop myself.* Seconds later, he sang for the first time in seven years; it was the hymn "His Eye Is on the Sparrow." His faith was restored, and it sounded mighty. I'm glad that the SOS from Heaven helped get him there! As a synchronicity side note, I'm a vocal advocate for supporting the work of our American troops, so I decided not to charge the man for our session. On his drive home, he got a flat tire. He was able to use the money he'd saved to help buy a new one. I think God had a hand in that one!

What's a Soul Like Yours Doing Outside a Body Like This?

I love stories about people who've had near-death and out-of-body experiences that took them to Heaven and back. The main difference is that NDEs usually happen during a traumatic event or surgery, and out-of-body experiences can occur when you're sleeping, meditating, daydreaming—basically in an altered state of consciousness.

I've found that NDE stories are rather consistent for such a rare occurrence. Most involve going through a tunnel, gravitating toward white light, and seeing loved ones who've already passed. Some people's souls are immediately enveloped in golden radiance. Others are guided to a brilliantly lit hall and feel total, absolute love. I've heard about visiting higher dimensions, with intelligence way beyond ours. There are also souls who get a tour of the after-life, while some don't get very far at all but encounter divine Spirit right away. Pat met a woman who had an NDE in her twenties as her body was experiencing complete organ failure. She said her soul entered a pitch-black space at first and then saw a window. Outside it was a male and female. The man appeared to be a bib-lical figure based on his appearance, dressed as he was in a robe and with a long beard. The female spirit was wearing a headscarf and seemed Eastern European. The woman didn't recognize either figure, but Pat's guess was that they were her guides. The woman then felt herself being drawn to the light on the other side of the window. Just as she approached it, she woke up.

Despite the hair-raising name, a near-death experience is always positive and life-affirming. A lot of times the person is pronounced dead until the soul returns, and it's deemed a miracle. When Spirit tells these souls that they have to return to their bodies, they're often disappointed. Can you blame them? Listen, God created a wonderful world for us here on earth, but in Heaven, it's perfection. Like mir-acles, I also think near-death experiences occur so that we can come back and teach others about them in the physical world. An NDE can also be a wake-up call to reevaluate your life and make changes. I've never had a near-death experience myself, but during readings, I've had Spirit tell me when a person has. A lot of times this happens when the clients doubt whether they really visited Heaven, and I'm meant to assure them that they did, and that they're not bananas.

Some people can have out-of-body experiences without severe harm to their health. This happened to Gram a few times, though she never made it all the way to Heaven. When Gram was preg-nant with my mom, she remembered fainting from anemia and seeing *her* grandmother who'd died. She was about to go to her, but she heard her mom calling her name and said to her grandma, "I gotta go! My mom's calling!"—and she came to. Many years later, Gram was lying on the sofa and felt her soul rise out of her body. When she told my mom about it, Mom said she could have had an out-of-body experience like astral projection, where the soul separates from the physical body and travels around. Shortly after, Gram was napping and felt like she was coming out of her body, this time from her back, and recognized what was happening. "Whoa, where do you think *you're* going?" she said to herself. With that, everything went back to normal.

God to You: "Mi Casa Es Su Casa!"

A lot of people talk about Heaven as God's home, but it's your immaculate dwelling too. Heaven is where we all come from and return to, and a lot of times when Spirit talks about people finally dying and traveling to the Other Side, they call it "going home." As someone who watches a lot of HGTV, I love hearing about how Heaven looks. God sounds like one heck of a decorator!

Those who've had near-death and out-of-body experiences are overwhelmed by the indescribable beauty, magnificence, and intensity of the Other Side. All the light, landscape, colors, and feelings the soul encounters—they're literally out of this world! Those who've experienced Heaven say there aren't even words to describe the feelings and sights, because we don't have the same things on earth, so the vocabulary that we use here falls short (God is described as so much more than we could ever explain too). Our language also can't fully depict what visitors remember about Heaven because you don't just feel, or see, or hear there—all of these things happen at once. Ideas aren't studied, they're "implanted," and even that makes it sound like a wacky sci-fi film, because they don't know how else to describe what they experience! I can relate to this frustration with words, though, because when I talk about what it's like to channel, I also have a hard time finding nouns, verbs, and adjectives to describe the sensations I feel and "know" to be true. It's like trying to draw a rainbow when you have only one crayon.

Heaven isn't just a productive pit stop between lives for us, or simply where God, angels, and other divine souls "live." It's a place where we feel intimately connected to His endless, perfect love. And because God is love, Heaven is a loving place. In Heaven, there's an all-embracing feeling that you belong, that you're treasured, and that you'll never feel judgment, blame, envy, fear, ego, anger, or other destructive emotions that you do here. People who've had NDEs talk about how they're overcome by feelings of acceptance, forgiveness, and a love more powerful than anything you could receive from your closest family, friends, and pets in the physical world, because it is so pure. And as you grow to levels closer to God, the energy frequency becomes more intense, as do these positive sensations. Though there are many levels and dimensions in Heaven, I don't know if it is above us or parallel to us, which is another topic that mediums debate. What matters is that Spirit is always within the warmest reach, whenever you need them.

Some of my favorite near-death stories describe Heaven as having dazzling, colorful landscapes with children playing, people singing and dancing, and animals scampering around. In church, I was taught that the streets are paved with gold, the gates are made of pearls, and the walls are decorated with sapphires, emeralds, rubies, topaz, amethyst, and other gems. I also think that Heaven may appear different based on what level you're on, and I wonder if it has unique features for everyone, depending on who experiences it, when, and for what purpose. I think of how various mediums can interpret messages and the afterlife differently, because they filter it through their own experiences and priorities. Maybe our interpretations of Heaven are customized in a similar way.

Remember the young boy Brian Murphy that I mentioned in chapter two, who died during a family vacation? Brian's father, Bill, keeps in touch with his soul in mind-boggling ways, and Brian's had a lot to say about God and Heaven. For one, Brian has told Bill that God is a "brilliant point of light, energy, and love that is beyond anything man will ever comprehend." And on many occasions, Brian's even taken Bill and his family on what Bill calls "soul journeys" that feel like very vibrant and surreal dreams, as they sleep. When telling each other about the dream the next day, each family member who went on the soul journey remembers the same details from it. During one trip, Brian's soul took Bill's to Heaven. Here's how Bill described it:

> *We walked through an enormous building similar to the Greek Parthenon. We passed angels that had radiant, golden auras who seemed to be filling out records. We then went out the back and there were children playing by a stream and waterfall. Everything was crystals and gems. The water was so clear, it seemed as if it wasn't even there. There was also the most beau-*

tiful singing, and it wasn't outside of me so that I was "listen-
ing" to it, but it was inside me and around me at the same time.
I could not tell you a direction it was coming from, but it made
me feel totally safe and at peace.

Brian went on to show Bill that there are different levels in Heaven, and said that the purpose of our existence on earth is to try to live a life that brings us closer to the next level and God, who is at the highest. Brian has also explained that he was an old soul that had lived in the physical world many times and reached a very high level. It's at these higher levels that you can interact more easily with earth, which is why Bill thinks Brian can take him on these journeys at all.

I see Bill and Regina for yearly sessions, and Brian has told me that he recently went to Jesus and asked if he could have a new responsibility—to help some children cross over, rather than having God send an angel. He said that the angels were so big and the children so small that the kids were sometimes frightened of the angels. Spirit told me that Jesus laughed and gave Brian the job. Okay, so I totally realize that last part doesn't have anything to do with what God or Heaven looks like, but I wanted to share it with you anyway, because I thought it was really neat.

Pray It Like You Mean It

Communicating with God can be personal and powerful. If you've never prayed before, I don't want you to be intimidated by it; prayer should feel like the most natural thing in the world, because God is in all of us. While meditating is listening to God, I think of prayer as asking God for what you desire. Spirit also refers to praying as "praising a higher power." Different faiths have various rituals that accompany prayer, and God honors all of them if they're done with a full heart and pure intent. Just because I say a Novena or the Rosary doesn't make me more religious or closer to God than you. And while I also believe God is the greatest source of healing and providing, Spirit tells me it's also okay to direct your requests to souls of faith, angels, guides, and even your loved ones. As you know by now, there are a lot of souls on the Other Side with divine abilities and contact with God. They work in conjunction with Him and can also "pick up the call"—though when you pray directly to God, I believe He's the only one that hears you.

During my prayers, I'm careful to always practice certain gracious habits. For example, no matter what I'm requesting, I do it with gratitude. Before I ask for whatever desire will fill my soul, I thank God for the blessings bestowed upon me. I also don't use the words "I want" or "I need"—at that rate, why not say, "Gimme gimme"? I ask God for his assistance in helping me to be patient, or to grant me the strength to behave during a testy situation. I also say "thank you" with the assumption that my request is already on its way to me, instead of saying "please," which sounds like begging. Showing gratitude before you receive a blessing also implies that you have faith that He'll deliver. I always pray as passionately as I can, so God knows the intensity of my needs, and finally, I'm crazy specific. I'm not sure why Spirit doesn't intuitively know what we want, but they don't. They're very literal-minded. Getting particular also helps me better understand what *I* do and don't want, so that I recognize the answer to my prayers when I see it.

So, for instance, let's say you'd like to meet Mr. Right. Your prayer wouldn't sound like, "Dear God, please send me a husband," or "Hey, God, can you send me a good man?" Instead you'd say, "Dear God, I want to thank you for my family, my work, my dog . . . I also want to thank you for introducing me to a man who's tall, dark, handsome, has no facial hair, is financially stable, loves and respects me . . ."—and so on. It's okay to yap God's ear off. He's a good listener!

If praying doesn't appeal to you, you can visualize what you desire instead. Maybe praying sounds too religious, or right now you're not talking to God because you're upset that a loved one died. Visualizing your needs is another way to send a message to the Other Side about what you long for, because you're in a meditative state that opens you to Spirit. You're also focusing on your heart's desire with a clear intent, similar to when you pray. To try visualization, sit quietly in a meditative state and empty your head. Surround yourself in white light and root yourself to the earth, like when you're meditating. Then, in your mind's eye, paint a specific picture of what you'd like.

Let's try an example. Say you want to expand your family. While sitting quietly, you'd visualize every aspect of that beautiful baby—from a healthy gestation, to a safe birth, to the child's arrival and transition into its new home and family. Engage all of your senses. Feel its fingers wrap around yours, smell its hair, picture the infant smiling up at you, hear it gurgle and coo, taste the child's skin when you kiss its tiny forehead. Repeat the visualization every day.

As for me, I like to be extra thorough and both pray *and* visualize at the same time for an ardent one-two punch. So when I want Victoria to be happy in college, for example, I pray to God to watch over her, and then I visualize Him protecting her in His incredible white light and Gram sitting on the bed to calm her. I see her getting to class on time, studying, having fun with friends, and making all the right choices about boys, school, and how to spend her money.

Another thing: because God gave you free will, you can't rely *only* on prayer and visualization without making an effort yourself. God's not your genie in a bottle, and magical thinking isn't Spirit's cue to give you what you want. As another for-instance, if you want support in a meeting, you need to prepare for it. What you would then pray and/or visualize is that your rehearsed words flow perfectly from your mouth with ease and grace, and that everyone hears you and is in awe of what you have to say. See the difference? You will when you start practicing these techniques!

Finally, it's good to pray for your loved ones who've crossed over. It's not the Catholic in me saying this; Spirit talks about it a lot too. Their souls know when you're speaking to them, and your prayers send them energy to help them on their journey on the Other Side. Thank them for their guidance and pray that their souls reach the highest attainable level of God's light and love. You don't even have to do this as an organized prayer; just thinking about them with love helps them as well. Consider it a way of "giving back" for all they do for you behind the scenes.

Spotted: Celebrities in Heaven

I've talked a lot about God and other well-known divine beings, but you'll also find celebrities on the Other Side. This shouldn't be too surprising, since they're departed souls of humans like you and me. *US Weekly* has always said that "Stars are just like us!" and

I've channeled the souls to prove it. We always read about how "They carry yoga mats!" and "They swim in pools!" Another valid caption? "They go to the Other Side!"

What's funny is that a lot of the celebs I've channeled have come through as a surprise. I didn't sit with the living family member of a famous person for a soul to show up. The souls made cameos in random people's readings on their own, which may say how accessible they are in the afterlife. I guess there's no velvet rope in Heaven!

I've had musicians step forward and make many meaningful points. First, there was Elvis. I read a woman, and her husband's soul came through to tell me that his family had a Christmas tree with all Elvis ornaments on it. So I said, "Who liked Elvis?" and the woman goes, "My husband was *obsessed* with him." Just then, I heard a voice say, "Elvis is really dead"—and I saw a blinged-out, white jumpsuit with bell-bottoms and a poof of black hair. The woman probably wished her husband were around to tell him the news, but since he was on the Other Side too, he already knew! Also, I read a girl in Howard Beach, New York, and I said, "Michael Jackson's soul is here and telling me that you have a T-shirt from his 1982 tour." The girl looked stunned. She was a huge fan. She said that she was wearing the shirt before she came, but changed it at the last minute. Michael then stepped forward to thank her for being a fan. Also, when he came to me, he didn't appear with one glove or how he looked toward the end of his life. Departed souls show themselves as either how you remember them or how they want to be remembered. Michael came as a child, and I interpret it as him always being an innocent soul.

Artists have come through to comfort the person I'm reading as well. The rapper Tupac stepped forward to console a guy whose friend died in a drive-by shooting, which is how Tupac died. There was also a girl who lost her mom, and Spirit wanted me to ask if she liked Whitney Houston. First I saw the mom's soul, and then I saw Whitney Houston wearing sunglasses with a scarf wrapped around her head, like in *The Bodyguard*. The girl said her mom wasn't Whitney's biggest fan or anything, so Spirit then showed me her mother driving in a car with Whitney, while the two sang "I Will Always Love You." The women were crying and laughing at the same time. With that, the girl gasped. "On our way here," she said, "me and my girlfriends were singing that song, laughing and crying hysterically." Not only was that her mom's way of telling the girl she was with her at that moment, but in Heaven, Mom was also with Whitney! The talented singer showed herself to me in a way that she wanted to be remembered—as a strong and beautiful woman who cares about her family and others.

Though it's always remarkable when famous souls drop in during a reading, I really enjoyed channeling a regal president. In Queens, New York, I read a guy who was tattooed, bearded, and tough-looking. In a quick flash, I saw Abe Lincoln's soul standing next to him. It was like, boom! Abe Lincoln! I told the guy that Abe was with us, and he flipped, because he wasn't only "a fan" of our sixteenth president but also one of those guys who did Civil War reenactments. Oddly enough, I've since heard of other Abe Lincoln Spirit sightings throughout Queens. Don't ask me why, though I know Lincoln and his wife were very spiritual, especially after their son William's death. But maybe Abe has a fondness for New York City's boroughs because when he died, his body was paraded through the streets in a funeral march on its way to his final resting spot in Springfield, Illinois. Or maybe he's just hanging around Arthur Avenue, hoping to scare up a cannoli.

Big-shot Spirit can also stop by for the heck of it. One of my favorite stars was so coy and charming when he came through that it really illustrates how you keep your personality in Heaven. I was drying my hair and about to take a call from the booker for *The Tonight Show with Jay Leno*. Out of nowhere, I wondered if Johnny Carson was dead. I yelled down to Larry, "Did Johnny Carson die?" and he goes, "Really, Theresa? Yeah, freaking Johnny Carson is dead." So I turned the blow dryer back on, and Johnny says to me, "You're going to my old studio."

Johnny then showed me a quick filmstrip of a skinny hallway lined with photos of old guests. When I got on the phone with Leno's booker, I said, "Hey, listen, Bob, I had a visit from Johnny Carson, and he's telling me that I'm going to his old studio with pictures lining the hall." But Bob said to me, "I don't know, Theresa. Johnny Carson did die, but we're in a new building. He never filmed *The Tonight Show* in this building, and we don't have hallways like that." So I thought, *Okay, that was awkward. But I guess I can't be right about everything!*

I did Leno, and it went fine. The next morning, I was on *Access Hollywood,* and as soon as I walked in, I saw a huge mural of Jay Leno with a hallway veering off, but I didn't go down it. I was getting my eyes and lips touched up just offstage and began channeling the makeup artist's brother who drowned. All of a sudden, Spirit literally pushed my face to look over to my left and into the dark, empty theater. Who do you think I saw? Johnny Carson, wearing a tan suit with brown shoes, reclining back with his feet up on the stadium seats. He was right in the middle of a row that was in the middle of the theater. I told everyone about it, but I was like, "What is Johnny Carson doing *here*?" One of them said that for about a year, he filmed *The Tonight Show* in the *Access Hollywood* studio. And that hall I told you about with the Jay Leno mural? If I'd continued down it to the breezeway area where they load equipment, I would have seen Johnny's mural on the other end. Spirit was practically announcing, "Heeere's Johnny!"

E Does Not Equal
MC Hammer

"Energy" is a science-y term that psychics like to use a lot, though I'm not sure many of us would say we missed our calling as professors or technology gurus. I've met my share of mediums, and I've never heard any of them confide, "Gosh, I really wanted to be a physicist, but I knew talking to dead people would make me more popular at parties." Are you out of your mind? If you handed me a radiometer, I'd probably use it as a paperweight. Even when the kids needed help with their science fair projects growing up, it was a group effort at our house—me, Larry, my parents, we'd all pitch in. And believe me when I say that I was rarely the one steering the rocket ship.

But I'm going to do my best to explain a little more about how energy relates to your body, your soul, and the afterlife in a way that's easy to understand. Up until now, I've talked about how God is energy, our souls are made of energy, and how our energetic vibrations get stronger as our souls grow and as we ascend to higher levels of Heaven. I've also discussed how souls with stronger energy communicate more clearly and with more personality. To tease out the rest of this topic, I'll try not to sound too academic or metaphysical, but if you have a thinking cap lying around, you may want to put it on. This might be a lot to process if you haven't had your coffee yet or thought about this stuff since high school.

So pay attention, students! The gist of today's lesson is this: everything is energy—it is at the core of what we see, do, and think about. Not only *are* we energy, but we also *use* our energy to tell the world who we are, what we care about, and who we aspire to be. I also believe that everything that exists in the universe is united by a collective energy that connects, promotes, and supports life and the afterlife. It is an amazing continuum that maintains how our bodies operate, how our souls evolve, and the way that our minds function and process emotion. Energy bonds us to each other and to God, because I believe energy comes from God, the creator of the whole shebang.

Aren't You Just a Ball of Energy?

Albert Einstein was a man of big ideas, and like me, even bigger hair. And one of the few things I remember and understood about him from science class when I was young is his equation: $E = mc^2$. It basically shows us that energy (E) and mass (m) can be converted into each other. What's more, the German physicist famously said, "Energy cannot be created or destroyed, it can only be changed from one form to another." Sounds intense and maybe a little confusing, but I think the easiest way to understand this concept is to think about the water cycle. There is a finite amount of water on our planet, and while that water can change form, it never disappears. It falls as rain, some is absorbed by plants and animals, and some evaporates back into the clouds to fall again. The water that is evaporated is eventually placed back in the environment by death or excrement, and the cycle repeats. This water is never created or destroyed—it just changes. Same goes with energy. It changes form, but it never disappears.

One way that E can change is from potential to kinetic energy. Potential is related to how an object stores energy, and kinetic is the energy of motion. A tank of gas has a certain potential energy that is converted to kinetic energy by the engine; when the potential is used up, you're out of fuel (and luck, if you're not near a gas station)! Or batteries, when they're new or recharged, have a certain potential. When I put them into a boom box and crank up the volume, the potential energy in the batteries is turned into kinetic energy to drive the speakers. When the potential energy is gone, the batteries are dead.

Like water, gas, and batteries, you can also use and change the energy in and around you, in a variety of ways. The body and soul are both energy, but in different forms. The human body is much heavier energy than your soul, which is lighter and more purified. Again, think of the water metaphor. H_2O can take the shape of a hard and solid ice cube, or it can be liquid or vapor. The human body is similar, in that its energy is transposed into a different form that's no longer dense but light. I'm not saying that your body dissolves into a soul when you die, but that both your soul and your body are energy in different forms.

A lot of people wonder why we even need a body, if we're energy in both the physical world and on the Other Side. Why not just pick a form of energy and stick with it, right? But your body here serves a purpose that's linked to the afterlife. You use it to make freewill choices, and you need all of its parts to experience life in the physical world. You need your body to move, and you also need it to feel the kinds of emotions that cause you to make choices and changes. Negativity, pain, sorrow, loss—your body and mind trigger these feelings, so that you can learn lessons that grow your soul. You know how Kelly Clarkson sings, "What doesn't kill you makes you stronger"? I'll do you one better. What doesn't kill you makes your soul wiser. You learn from hard situations and use them to inform future ones. On the Other Side, Spirit says it's mostly rainbows and Skittles, so your soul can't learn things with the same impact that it does here.

The way your body can affect your soul, plus its ability to overcome setbacks and lead to self-awareness, is a powerful use of collective energy. During a show in Louisville, Kentucky, I met a sixteen-year-old boy named Reese. He has cystic fibrosis and lost his father to a fatal heart attack at age five. The two were very close— Dad took his son to the office every day, and after he died, Reese kept his black shirt, which was the last one he ever wore in this world. Reese had been through hell with feeding tubes, hospitals, surgeries, and funeral homes. He'd also been to therapists, because so much pent-up sadness and frustration fueled anger issues that caused Reese to beat up on his siblings. When I asked Reese what his name was, I actually thought he said it was "Grease." You know what he said to that? "Strike one, you got that wrong." Feisty bugger. But his father's soul came through to say how proud Reese makes him and how impressed he is with how much he does for his community. (I later found out that Reese has a bucket list of ways he wants to make people's lives easier, including delivering meals to families in need and raising money for Christmas gifts for children's hospital patients.) After the reading, Reese's mother told me that her son had let go of his rage and stopped hitting his brother. "He knows his dad is watching him," she said, laughing. "In his head, Dad's telling him to be nice." But without the physical and emotional challenges that caused Reese to struggle all these years, he wouldn't have room to grow. Trials sure feel unfair at the time, and I'm not celebrating that this poor kid has gone through so much, but without them, he wouldn't see the value of paying it forward and healing more souls than his own—and that's a significant opportunity for a young man.

There are also countless blessings of living in a physical body, because God wants us to enjoy our time here, both by ourselves and with each other. He's not a Tiger God, determined to be strict, practical, and overly focused on learning and achievement. For one, He's given your body five senses, because they can bring you amazing happiness if you stop to recognize them as they occur. Petting your dog, kissing your partner, eating a slice of lemon meringue pie, smelling a hydrangea, watching the snow fall, hearing a child laugh—all of these things are a warm hug for your soul. The joy your body feels from these experiences can also turn into kinetic energy. It can put pep in your step or make you smile, ear to ear. God's also given us a sacred planet, and we need to use our body's energy to appreciate, respect, and protect it while we're here. We always talk about taking care of the environment for our children, but considering that Spirit says our souls eventually reincarnate, doing this will benefit your own future lifetimes too.

Another way that you can use your body is to express yourself, your gifts, and the essence of your soul. Singers physically share their souls by using their diaphragms and vocal cords, sculptors do it by using their hands, and fashionistas do it by dressing their bodies. My husband, Larry, expresses himself with the tattoos he gets inked onto his body. He loves animals and birds—the man's skin looks like a poster you'd buy at a zoo gift shop. He has a tattoo of a koi fish, which is a symbol of perseverance and the fact that he's always striving to improve and succeed in life; Larry has a dragon, which represents the way he protects his family; he has an eagle, which stands for freedom; and his rooster signifies his fighting spirit and the way he pushes himself to do better and succeed when people or obstacles get in his way. Larry also has a Harley-Davidson tattoo to show his passion for the motorcycle he loves to ride, and his newest 007 tattoo illustrates my husband's sense of humor. It's just like the one Daniel Craig had when he parodied Larry on *SNL*!

Send a Thoughtful E-Greeting

Souls who've crossed over don't need a physical body to transfer their energy; they make me sense and feel things by transferring their thoughts, feelings, and messages to me. Your thought vibrations are also powerful energy, and you can use them to manifest your ideas and attract your desires. Speaking and writing have the same effects, because those actions also begin with thoughts. I believe that the energy of our thoughts influences our lives and those of others, and they also attract the circumstances and people who share our mind-set. Our thoughts can help determine our success, outlook on life, and the company we keep. Spirit listens to your passionate and specific thoughts, whether they happen during meditation, prayer, or anytime you're focused on an idea, even if you're not consciously meditating but zoned out while driving a car or running on a treadmill. If you add a feeling to that energy, it becomes stronger and moves quicker.

Because you transfer energy with every interaction you make, be aware of the emotions that swish around in your mind and soul. Negative feelings like anger, hatred, or jealousy will create a circumstance just as quickly as if you put a positive feeling of love, joy, or excitement behind your intentions. Of course, there are a range of emotions in between—indifference, concern, hesitation—and that energy will boomerang back to you as well. Have you ever woken up on the wrong side of the bed, and watched your spouse soak up your apathy or grumpiness? It's like the person's soul is a big, absorbent kitchen sponge. Or do you ever start the day in a crummy mood, but immediately feel better after having coffee with a friend who tells hilarious stories? If a foul attitude can transfer energy just as much, and as fast, as laughter or friendliness, it helps to pay attention to your mood shifts and choose your company wisely.

When you focus your intentions by bringing energy to them, you turn them into action and create your reality. Your thoughts make up your actions, and thereby the reaction is created. This result can have endless repercussions, good or bad. I also think that maintaining consistent, upbeat energy helps make life a lot easier. If your energy is strong and balanced, things will move more positively in your direction and your soul will feel more fulfilled. When your energy is dysfunctional and fragmented, your flow becomes blocked or disturbed, and you'll face more challenges. Your energy here also affects your soul in the afterlife, because your life is assessed based on whether your actions (prompted by thoughts) had a positive or adverse effect on others.

When gifted healers do healings, they transfer all kinds of energy to their clients. They use thermal, or heat, energy, which is the physical manifestation of God's energy surging through their bodies (some healers' hands actually turn red and feel hot). They also heal with thought energy by using their minds to call on their, and your, guides and angels; then they merge the energy from these beings with their own energy to assist in curing the problem. They think about what the physical or emotional issue is and how they'd go about fixing it as well; those directed thoughts and intentions help promote wellness. And because so much energy comes from thinking, they can do healings in their home or remotely. It works the same way and with similar speed and efficiency.

Your body language can also give off energy, because that too is initiated with thought. I've had clients who ooze emotion, whether it's bitterness, fear, vulnerability, or sadness. They transfer energy just by how they cross their arms, bite their inner cheek, or can't look me in the eye. It doesn't take a spiritual gift to sense or be affected by it.

We always credit our brains with turning our thoughts into words and actions, but so many thoughts begin at the soul level. On the Other Side, our souls speak through thought and we are infinitely and energetically connected to that part of ourselves. I've found that my own brain can be unreliable sometimes, so I trust that a lot of what I say comes from a more instinctual place. But I'll bet you've also had eureka moments where you've surprised yourself with a really insightful or uncharacteristic conclusion and wondered, *Did that just come out of my mouth?* Those moments often start in the soul.

Put Your Vibes Up

All energy has a vibration, but when it comes to understanding what *your* energy's vibration is, it's helpful to think of a ceiling fan and its blades. When it is not in operation, you're going to see five stationary blades. That's like your vibration as a human being because you are very solid, heavy energy. When you turn the fan on, the blades begin to disappear and the vibration/speed is very quick; it looks like the blades are one movement. That's how Spirit's vibration is. It's much faster than ours, since souls are very light and can move faster.

I also know the frequency on the Other Side is different, because I can feel the shift when souls remove themselves from that dimension and change their vibrations to be among us. Because of this energy change, I have to raise my vibration when I channel, and in my everyday life. One way to do this is to boost my spiritual integrity by practicing forgiveness, having compassion, and exercising less judgment.

Raising one's vibration isn't just a medium thing—it should be something you strive to do too. It will help you connect with loved ones in a better way, and it will benefit your everyday life. Everyone's energy has a vibration that changes depending on who's around you, what your mood is, and what foods and substances you put into your body. We should all want to vibrate at the highest level we can. When you raise your vibration, you affect both the body and soul. The more positive your vibration is in the physical world, the more lessons you are learning and working through, and as a result, your soul elevates. Everything works hand in hand.

Pat taught me that great ways to raise your vibration in the here and now include gratitude, laughter, music, prayer, meditation, and dance; these positive activities also attract good energy back to you. You can also raise your vibration with uplifting visualizations and breathing exercises. Surrounding yourself with a color you love—in a room you spend a lot of time in, or by putting on a brightly colored shirt—can lift your spirits and shift your vibration too. It's no coincidence that I'm in a better mood when I wear canary yellow shoes, dance around to Train, play a joke on my kids, feel grateful for my friends, and fit prayer and meditation into my day. It's total bliss to raise my vibration. An instant high!

Vibrations increase with positivity, and as yours rises, just watch: you'll become more sensitive to other people and the environment you're in. You may start to sense if someone is in pain or struggling, be it physically or emotionally. I think this is why my husband, Larry, cries so easily since I accepted my gift. He's become more empathetic from coming to most of my group readings and from being at my shows. He feels people's emotions more intuitively and intensely than before, and he naturally finds himself doing more good for others, since he sees how it impacts us here and in Heaven. Those ASPCA commercials make him sob like crazy, he engages the most unlikely characters in emotional conversations (most recently, heavy metal bassist Rudy Sarzo!), and when Larry hears a child sing opera on *America's Got Talent*, the guy leaves water marks on my sofa. We recently met Oprah Winfrey at a party hosted by Discovery Communications, Inc. (they own TLC, which airs *Long Island Medium*), and he actually told her he "cried like a baby" during the farewell episode of her ABC talk show. Oprah being Oprah, she squeezed his hand sympathetically. I sure hope Larry's vibration has gone way up, or else my husband's just getting soft in his old age!

Instant Attraction: Energy and Objects

I've seen energy and Spirit cling to personal objects like Saran Wrap. Items made from fabric (clothes, blankets, scarves) and solid things like jewelry, especially with stones, attract and hold energy long after a person is no longer wearing or using them. A lot of clients bring objects with them to a reading or show, but I don't have to touch them to feel their energy; Spirit just tells me when I should mention them and tells me what to say. I've had a loved one's soul tell me to acknowledge that a woman was wearing her mom's cremains as a necklace, to validate its presence. I wouldn't have known otherwise; it was just a silver chain with a pendant. Personally, I find it comforting to keep my loved ones' favorite objects, and therefore energy, close to me. I wear Gram's wedding ring a lot, especially to big events like my son's lacrosse games or Victoria's gymnastics meets. I'm always missing Gram, so I like to bring her with me wherever I can. When I feel her energy, I feel her presence.

Since energy can't be destroyed, it can remain as an impression or vibration in inanimate objects. So when I bring new stuff into my house, especially antiques and estate jewelry that have a history, I always sage and encircle them in God's white light. Energy is also drawn to wood, so I give furniture and mirrors more attention than most. Even if I buy new household goods like appliances,

I sage and surround them with light, because the item could have been in an old warehouse with bad energy, or the person handling it may have had unpleasant energy attached to him or her. Trust me, the wrong type of energy is a free gift you don't want!

The craziest example I have of an object holding on to energy is my friend Marie's wooden end table that moved across her room when I visited. I'm sure you remember it from the show. The heirloom belonged to Marie's grandparents. Marie and her friends used to play with it when they were kids. They'd ask the table questions, and tell it to knock once for yes, twice for no . . . and it did! Marie's grandmother was very spiritual, and at one point, she felt something bad was going to happen to her eighteen-year-old granddaughter. She told her family that she didn't want to use the table anymore, not even for fun, because she felt it was going to tell her who was going to die. Her granddaughter did die soon after, and they never used the table again.

Marie's table was stored in her sister's basement, but she took it out for the first time in thirty years to show it to me. We wanted to see if the table would move for us, the way it did for Marie's family when she was young. So I saged the table, protected it in God's light, and asked for only the highest good of all concerned. If I was going to put my hands on that piece of furniture, I wanted to make sure its energy was purified!

Me, Marie, her mom, and her brother Michael sat on all four sides of the table and lightly put our hands on it. The table vibrated. I then asked everyone to lift their hands just above the table (I didn't want people watching the show to think we were moving it). Right then, the table began to slowly slide and *slightly lift up*; then, it moved across the floor really fast toward Michael.

We didn't push or pull the table with our hands, there was no fishing wire attached to move it from off-camera, and the floor was perfectly level in Marie's home. I've never seen anything like it before or after! Marie said she and other visitors have tried to make the table move since, but it won't stinkin' budge.

So what kind of energy made the table move? You got me. I knew Marie's grandmother's soul was present for protection, but I didn't sense that she was moving the table or that other Spirit made the piece glide either. The energy was something I didn't recognize, and it was *in* the table. I also didn't sense it was negative energy. I had my hesitations about airing the scene, because I thought nobody would believe it. But do you know how many emails I got saying, "Growing up, we had a table just like that"? Stop it!

Negative Energy—Do Not Enter

If you've just flipped ahead, hoping to read a bunch of spooky tales about possessions, hauntings, and *American Horror Story*–type encounters, the next few pages may be a letdown. In fact, this may be the least scary chapter on negativity you'll ever read in a book about dead people! The reason is because I don't deal with negative Spirit, and if they're around, I barely acknowledge them, much less interact with them. I have a similar MO when it comes to destructive people—I choose not to engage. But I can't completely ignore the fact that negative people and negative Spirit exist, and they may be upsetting you, so I want to share my thoughts, experiences, and two cents on the topic. Just because I don't like negative energy doesn't mean I don't have an opinion about it.

In the last chapter, I briefly talked about how negative attracts negative, and positive attracts positive, in terms of transferring thought energy. But it's important to also see how these vibrations manifest in the actual people, situations, and Spirit in your life. Spirit wants you to surround yourself with positive influences and spend less time in negative situations. I think this is because positivity benefits soul growth, and Spirit is really good at seeing the big picture and not just enjoying instant gratification. If there weren't a long-term perk to being positive, Spirit would suggest we cheer ourselves up by eating a Philly cheesesteak when we're sad or stressed out!

When you're upbeat and make an effort to raise your vibration all the time, it's natural for good souls who've gone into the light to be drawn to your positive energy. They will surround, guide, and protect you, because they come from God, who is also good. But when you are fearful, destructive, or dysfunctional, then your home and life can be a very comfortable place for negative Spirit to thrive. Negative souls are immature and all too eager to feed off your fear and vulnerability—just like a deceitful, selfish, mean, or unreliable person in this world would. Not surprisingly, such low-level energies were not on the up and up in the physical world either. Their souls have a lot of learning to do before they advance on the Other Side, and they can spend a lot of time trying to get your attention and throw off your better intentions. But just as a close friend would suggest that you guard yourself from negative people by establishing boundaries, illuminating positivity, not harping on a bad moment, and seeing life through a glass half full, you need to do the same by guarding yourself from unscrupulous Spirit.

People Who Need Positive People

I realize that having a good attitude is no easy feat, especially when you're busy, stressed, grieving, or all of the above, but your soul doesn't need to go from Archie Bunker to Little Miss Sunshine overnight. You'll need to make an effort to establish and then maintain a good attitude, but it's worth it. It reminds me of how both my kids had braces and the tiniest adjustments to their crooked teeth eventually led to the most beautiful smiles. Then after the braces came off, they had to wear retainers to make sure their teeth didn't go back to their old ways. Similarly, small shifts in perspective can make a big impact, and surrounding yourself with positivity is like having a retainer for your soul.

Look around, and I'll bet you'll have no problem finding examples of how attitude adjustments made life easier and more fun. For me, it happens every day on the set of our show. I don't have a lot of rules for the *Long Island Medium* crew to follow when they come into my home, but one is that they address everyone by name and say good morning to him or her. This sets the tone for the day and makes it enjoyable to come to work. I don't always wake up with a grin, but small gestures like this brighten my outlook too.

Your attitude toward the weather is another detail that can affect your day. Rain, for example, can drown a cheerful attitude in no time. You don't need to have a phobia about it like I did to hate how it causes traffic jams, makes your hair frizz, and ruins white pants. But to keep from getting down, you know what I do? I think of the walk I'll take when the sun comes out. And with heavier situations, like the death of a loved one, I won't belittle your feelings by saying you should get over it by going for a stroll. Your process is going to be different from mine or the next person's, and healing can take a while. But as you work through any situation, I find that having a hopeful outlook on smaller nuisances, like the weather, lets you pay more attention to handling the stuff that really matters. The fickle climate becomes one less thing you have to worry about.

A lot of times, just anticipating a bad person or situation can create negative energy in you, well before the encounter ever happens. I know a woman whose mother-in-law crawls under her skin for at least a week before she's due to see her. She gets a stomachache, starts petty fights with her husband, stomps around the house—all this because she expects to feel attacked by her mother-in-law's criticism in the near future. But by getting her dander up ahead of time, the woman transfers her sour expressions to family and friends, and in some ways creates her own reality. Instead of huffing around, I suggested that she visualize the two families having a great time together and imagine her handling her mother-in-law's insults in an effortless way. This sends a message to Spirit about the kind of guidance she needs. She can also be practical about prepping for the visit by coming up with replies ahead of time. The truth of the matter is that other people can help make us happy, but they're not responsible for our happiness—we are.

Spirit often suggests a great exercise to those carrying negative emotions connected to a person's death, but I think it's useful for any negative situation, really. They'll say, "Visualize me standing in front of you, with a suitcase open at my feet. Please put all the negative burdens that you carry connected to my passing inside, close the suitcase, and hand it back to me with love. These are my burdens to carry, not yours." So the next time you find yourself in a dire situation, I recommend that you try this visualization: put everything you wish you could say and do to that person into a large suitcase, close it (will it even shut?), and hand it back with love. We spend way too much time carrying other people's baggage, and it's time to send 'em packing.

Why Negative Entities Don't Scare Me

Just as I don't devote much energy to negative people, I also don't spend time worrying about negative Spirit. I feel that the less I fear and acknowledge these entities, the less I will interact and connect with them. And I like to think that as a result, this is one reason I've personally never encountered demons, poltergeists, or other evil beings that scurry along roofs or possess people that can't seem to ignore their presence. But just because I don't deal with this bad Spirit, doesn't mean that I doubt they exist. I didn't experience the Holocaust or Great Potato Famine, but I don't question that *those* events were real.

I think you're more in control of negative Spirit than books, shows, and films let on. I always ground and protect myself in God's light, regularly sage, and when I channel, I ask for the highest good of all concerned and souls that walk with God. It's when you don't protect yourself and you feed into negativity that I think it can multiply. If your bed shakes for no reason, you can shut it down with saging and prayer, or you can encourage it with a certain level of fascination. If your cat skids across the floor as if it were kicked, you can research a priest and medium to get rid of the nuisance that caused it, or you and your friends can provoke the energy to do it again. You know what I mean?

Not too long ago, I did a show in Vegas and met this gruff, mustached, biker guy, and Spirit told me that he had abilities like mine. I asked him if this was true, and he said, "No, it's not the same. I only see evil. I turn on the TV and can see who's a child molester, or watch the news and know if someone's guilty of murder. I don't understand how you only see positive energy, when I only see negativity." Okay, I have two points to make about this conversation. First, I can also watch a *Dateline* investigation and know who the killer is, but that's not where my thinking ends. I intuitively find whatever good there might be in the situation—maybe the victim's family became closer after her death, or the story raised awareness about gun control laws. I then say a quick prayer for the victim and for the family to know that the person is at peace. That is, I make a concerted effort to raise my vibration, to help buffer a negative event, for everyone's benefit.

Second, delivering healing messages from positive Spirit is a choice. During the show that the biker guy saw, all I delivered were positive messages—I did not sense or feel anything negative whatsoever, even though this man said that he did. In fact, I channeled a young girl whose boyfriend murdered her, and she left behind a son. Clearly this was a horrible, tragic, negative thing that happened, but I didn't get gruesome or gory details from Spirit. Instead, the girl's soul came forward to tell her family that she took responsibility for dating a man they never trusted, and she wanted them to let the authorities handle his punishment and focus instead on caring for her child. She brought the family comfort by letting them know she was okay and admitting that she put herself in a harmful situation, so that they wouldn't feel any guilt related to her passing.

So I'm not saying there aren't negative energies out there, because you can't have good without bad, and people make terrible decisions all the time, some of which may be influenced by negative entities. But you can control how much you let into your life and soul. Incidentally, Spirit also suggested that I tell the negative Spirit man that he could change the information he received if he wanted, but he just gave me a look like, "That's easier said than done, lady." And that's fine, because I'm certainly not the last word on this topic, but the encounter made me think about how we all make conscious choices to frame a situation in a positive or negative light, and how it can affect our well-being.

Positive and Negative Energy in Your House

Since everything we touch holds on to some level of positive or negative energy, your homes and the land they're built on are no exception. And because Spirit is energy, they linger too. Older homes can have more energy and Spirit than newer ones, because they've been around longer and acquired more of a history—more activities, events, and people passing in and out of them. New construction also has energy, likely from the land or your own departed loved ones dropping by for the afternoon.

If Spirit lingers in your home, people automatically assume this is haunting, negative energy, but it doesn't have to be. Because a soul can get attached to a building or property, it might choose to stay in the house, but more likely, the soul is visiting from Heaven and not there all the time. I know a man who occasionally sees the soul of the guy who once owned his home. The first time this happened, the soul told him not to be afraid and explained that he built the house and likes to see other families enjoy it as much as his did. If this guy didn't have such an openly communicative soul on his hands, it would be easy to assume that his place was scary, because let's face it, not everyone has a dead guy hanging out in their living room, and most movies tell us that when there's a Spirit around, it's bad. But this soul meant no harm, and the man asks for his privacy whenever he wants it. I suspect the soul also enjoys being around this man because he too is a lovely person. Would he have preferred that his house come with a spare bedroom or bonus closet? Sure, but there was no harm in getting good Spirit either.

Sometimes when I walk into a home, Spirit will tell me what was on its land before the house was built—be it a farm, sacred burial ground, what have you—and if the energy that still resides there is positive or negative. During a private reading, Spirit told me that the home's owner was genuinely upset about some trees that were chopped down in her backyard. She feared that she disrupted the land because under the trees were tombstones, and the company she hired to remove the trees got rid of everything! She was afraid the souls buried there would be angry and threaten her peaceful house, but a few of them actually stepped forward to say that since it wasn't her fault that the graves were removed and she wasn't building on the land, she shouldn't worry. In fact, they found her sincerity a plus, and I suspect they'll help keep her home safe from here on out.

Homes that have experienced intense positive and negative emotion can hold on to that energy, but it doesn't have to last forever. I once did a reading for a couple in their house, which was newly renovated and felt positive to me. But as I walked through it, in my mind's eye I saw flashes of walls splattered in blood, and I even got a tinny blood taste in my mouth. I also saw a priest standing in the corner. This all startled me at first, but I was there to do my job and didn't want to scare the couple by mentioning what I saw and sensed, so I went ahead with the reading. I should have known Spirit wouldn't ignore the elephant in the room! During the session, they said the husband was a cheapskate, showed me yellow tape around the house, and told me that people had brutally died in that space. I shared this with the couple, and the wife validated that when they bought the house, they got it really cut-rate because a family was murdered in it and nobody wanted it. They'd gutted the house and had a priest bless it, and Spirit confirmed that it was now free of bad energy. But even though they'd ripped down most of the walls, the space still held that imprint for me. I couldn't, however, feel anything menacing in it—the priest had taken its palpable energy away.

Know too that the energy and Spirit *you* bring into your home can matter most of all. If your home feels happy or heavy, take a good look at your own life before you go blaming the previous owners or some dead lady's soul that you swear is haunting the attic. Then grab that sage and start smudging. The best thing about sage is that it doesn't work just on Spirit. It breaks up all kinds of negative energy. When I'm in an off mood or after an annoying visitor is at the house, I like to sage while saying a positive affirmation like, "We only have room in this house for peace, love, joy, and contentment. We don't have room for negative thoughts, feelings, or emotions—please go to the light."

Standing Up to Negative Spirit

More often than not, I've found that when people casually tell me that their home is "haunted" by a scary spirit, the space is really occupied by a nice soul that hasn't been given boundaries. It's like that hotel we filmed at for the show that was called the Padre Hotel in Bakersfield, California; here, a little girl's soul told me that she and other Spirit watch over the place and like to sing and dance in the halls. These souls weren't negative, but they do cause a ruckus, and if you're not a fan of unexplained noises, that can seem scary. Less common is when a negative soul disrupts or haunts the living in a bad way, in which case, it's important to call a medium or priest to efficiently handle it.

Since I've never encountered a negative nuisance, I dug into Pat's bag of stories for an example. Years ago, she helped a very mean and aggressive soul cross over. He was upsetting a ten-year-old girl who lived in a home that he'd occupied for many years. As Pat began to direct him to the light, he resisted her with such energy that it began to slowly push against her body until she bent backward. She spread her feet to anchor herself. It wasn't painful, just uncomfortable, and she won. Pat called him a coward, and he broke. She'd brought a medium that could see and hear the soul, and the soul said he was afraid to meet his maker because of bad stuff he'd done to his own kids and the fact that he was now scaring this child. Knowing he was vulnerable, Pat then called his mother's soul forward on the Other Side, and she came for her son and helped him cross.

Ultimately, a lot of what made this negative soul back down is that Pat and the medium weren't scared. As I've said before, fear is your worst enemy, regardless of whether you're dealing with people who are dead or alive. Bill Murphy, the father of the little boy Brian I've talked about who drowned, said something interesting to me the other day about this. He has noticed a common theme among those on TV who claim that their homes and lives are inhabited by evil Spirit:

One of the most interesting things I have gotten out of watching these negative type shows about demons and evil is that the people undergoing this problem all seem to have homes filled with an overload of religious items—pictures, statues, angels, crucifixes, you name it. I'm not talking about signs of faith, but artifacts that are kept because people are afraid. Fear is a negative feeling and will bring about negative results, so I think a lot of the problems they encounter may be fed by their response to it. If your fear of evil is greater than your belief in God as an all-powerful being, I suspect negative Spirit can feed off it.

If you ever do find yourself feeling uncomfortable or afraid in a way that you suspect is Spirit-related, surround yourself in a bubble of God's white light and protection and repeat, "This is not your space. In the name of God, you must leave." I also suggest the Our Father as a universal prayer of protection, no matter what religion you are. Keep saying either one until the sensation ends. It's essential that you don't have fear when you do this, so treat an exasperating entity with the kind of determination you usually save for annoying salesmen who won't leave your front door. Remember too that if you sense something that seems ominous, you'll be able to tell that it's coming from a bad place because of the messages and thoughts you'll receive. Tricky energy will tell you what to do, while a soul that's visiting from Heaven will offer you guidance. Guidance is loving and beautiful, and it nudges you in a certain direction with encouragement. Also, souls that have gone into the light are thoughtful about letting you know they're around with signs, coincidences, and other gentle hellos. They're not out to scare you, and if you ask them to scram or take a beat, they most certainly will.

Spirit insists that while there's evil in all of the universes, there is much, much more good out there. Without some negativity, there'd be nothing for free will to rail against, no opportunities for our souls to evolve. In the epic war of good versus evil—in the universe, in your soul, and among PTA moms at your child's elementary school—love *always* conquers all.

Wanna Tour a Creepy Jail or Sad, Old House? Me Neither.

People often ask me if I have negative experiences at deserted mental institutions, old brothels, or poorly maintained inns. What kind of vacations do you think I take? As a rule, I don't intentionally tour or visit locations where I know depressing or brutal activities occurred, like Charles Manson's house or Sylvia Plath's crawl space. Given what I do and feel, why would I want to spend my free time there? It wouldn't make for a breezy afternoon off.

I have enjoyed going to more positive historic locations. When I was a kid, I was drawn to Teddy Roosevelt's house on the north shore of Long Island. It's called Sagamore Hill and has wide porches and amazing views of the Sound. It's very peaceful, and I always felt intrigued when I was inside. I remember that the furniture, especially in one of the bedrooms, felt very familiar to me. I recall seeing a table and thinking, *That's not right. There used to be a lamp there.* Because I didn't focus too much on my gift at the time, I also remember seeing a maid setting a table with doilies and now realize that she was a Spirit. I could also see myself sitting at one of the desks and writing with a quill pen. I don't know if this means that my soul lived in this house or lived in a home *like* this in the late 1800s, but either way, it's a fun thing to consider.

I also go to historic locations by accident when I'm on tour, because I do a lot of shows at old venues—and the energy in each is a crapshoot. I was in one old theater in Albany, where I saw a woman's soul on the balcony, and she told me, "I died here." Thanks for that, but I didn't want to know anything more. Another time, I felt a tap on my shoulder before a show, and when I turned around and saw that nobody was there, I heard a male soul's friendly laughter. It then said, "I touch *him* all the time too. Look to your left." That's when I saw a burly security guard next to me, minding his own business. I told him what happened, and he said, "Yeah, I get tapped! I've never told anyone that!" Finally, there was the show in Philadelphia where my iPhone began taking photos by itself. One shot was eerie and looked like either a distorted version of my face or like another person's face was on top of mine. Was this positive or negative energy? I don't know, though whatever it was had a good time fooling around with me. But I wasn't afraid, because I know that I and the guests at my shows are all protected.

Caught Between a Rock and a Heavenly Place

I feel I only channel souls that are already in Heaven, so as far as I know, I haven't worked with a "stuck soul" as a professional medium. However, I'm told that every once in a while, troubled Spirit may not want to leave the physical world after their bodies die, so they insist on staying here. While some stuck energies are negative, most are good souls that are misplaced, confused, and/or lost. It's like post-traumatic stress disorder for Spirit, and the souls aren't sure what to do next.

With stuck energy, the soul refuses to cross because of an unresolved problem that's left an impression on its consciousness.

For instance, the soul may not realize that its body is dead. It can also be the soul of a person who passed tragically and wants to tell its side of the story, so it stays put until it can. Some stuck Spirit believe the deeds they committed in the physical world were so unforgivable that they don't want to face God. This last scenario can happen with suicide victims, because of certain religious beliefs they held in their lifetime (not because their death was inexcusable). Other souls stay because they're waiting for a loved one, like a child for its mother or a spouse its partner.

This makes it sound like you have a choice about whether you go to the light, but it's more like, when you die, your soul goes there *unless* you're confused or choose not to. For stuck souls, crossing over requires assistance from higher beings and/or people on earth, including mediums that make it their mission to do this. I remember Pat telling me a story about how she and others with mediumship abilities worked with a man who was murdered, and his soul said that someone had covered up his death to make it look like the man killed himself. The soul was stuck, because he wanted his family to know that he did not commit suicide. He wanted to tell his side of the story. After several visits with his soul and communicating his messages to his family, he said he had to move into the light, because he had work to do. Pat and her cohorts helped him do this.

Though some suicide victims can get stuck, this isn't because they're not allowed into Heaven. I'll tell you right now that most of the souls who've committed suicide that I channel are at peace, but some do refuse to cross over because they're needlessly worried. Suicide is not part of the journey God set out for you to have; nobody is destined to prematurely end his or her time here to learn a lesson. But I do believe our guides assess suicide on a case-by-case basis—for example, taking your life because you're in physical pain, mentally ill, or dealing with an addiction can hardly be considered "taking the easy way out." But this is what souls can fear, because they're raised with religious beliefs that condemn them and this tragedy. I remember Pat telling me how she helped cross over a boy who fled from the light because he believed God would be upset that he killed himself. The soul followed around a high school classmate who had mediumship abilities, and when he refused to cross, she and some friends formed a prayer circle and told the boy that he could go, and he would not be condemned. He did, and he wasn't.

It's not for me to say what guides discuss with these souls during a life review, but Spirit does tell me they will need to explain why they left the world so early. And then, like the rest of us, they'll be held accountable for the lessons they didn't learn and the choices they could have made instead, and then revisit those teachings in a different, future life. They will also experience the pain of those they left behind, like we all do. I've compared living in the physical world to an internship or semester abroad—a way to learn lessons in a real-world capacity. But if you were to cut out of these types of programs early, you'd have to explain yourself to your counselors and be held accountable for what you missed. It's the same deal in Heaven, if you take your own life. But there's no punishment or ruler slapping for suicide, if that's what you're wondering. What's more challenging, perhaps, is that the souls who exit early feel regret, remorse, and have to come to terms with what their suicide means for their soul's growth and Karma (souls don't get "sad" like we do, but setbacks always make an impression). In addition to praying for your loved ones who've departed, I also encourage you to pray for suicide victims, even if you don't know one. This isn't because they need our prayers to bring them mercy or anything like that. We should use our positive energy to pray for them because our supportive thoughts give their souls some oomph to grow and evolve.

Three Not-So-Little Words:
Health, Grief, and Healing

No matter how amazing Spirit is about communicating with laughter and personality, my clients always cry when they're connecting with a loved one. How can they not? During a session, you feel intimately connected to those who've crossed over, and their messages tend to circle three subjects that speak to everyone's souls. I'm talking about the themes of health, grief, and healing, which run through all of my readings, because Spirit says that how you handle each one will impact the time you spend here and in the afterlife.

Health, grief, and healing are more connected than you might realize. Consider: Something causes your loved one's body to stop functioning—be it an accident, disease, or trauma (health). After that person dies, you mourn the loss (grief), and I believe that how effectively you do this can influence your mental, physical, and spiritual well-being (healing). You will always grieve for your loved ones, but it's important that your body and soul recover from their passing. If you don't heal, I feel that the stress, emotional upset, and trauma you hold inside can contribute to illness. Your grief can also affect your soul's growth if it's not released, because the burden keeps you from developing in this life and can be carried into the next.

So I'd like to discuss the various aspects of health, grief, and healing, because these topics are central to all of our lives and souls. Even if you are not actively mourning a loved one right now, you bought my book for a reason, and I don't think there are many accidents in our world. Maybe you were meant to read this today, come back to it another time, or earmark it for a friend. No matter what, I'll bet it's just what Spirit ordered.

Health: Why, Why, Why?!

If I had a dime for every time I said, "Why is this happening?" after a loved one got sick or passed away, Gram would never have to send me those silver coins again. I think that one of the hardest things to accept when you're in any tough, life-changing situation, particularly related to mortality, is that there aren't explanations to every question you have. I don't even know all the answers, and I've got a direct line to Heaven! But as you heal, one of the best gifts you can give yourself is permission to accept that there are some things you're not meant to know until you can ask around on the Other Side. Until then, repeat after me: "I'll find out when I get there." But I do want to share what Spirit's said about health and illness, so you can digest it in a way that means something to you.

Their points might even relate to a health issue *you're* experiencing right now.

So, based on what Spirit tells me, we contract many of our illnesses or health conditions so that we, and/or those around us, can learn from them. I often think of Michael J. Fox and how I'd never heard of Parkinson's before he made his condition public, nor did I know about pancreatic cancer until I watched Patrick Swayze fight it. These actors might not have advocated and done so much for those specific diseases if they weren't personally invested in their progress. An illness might also teach you discipline, patience, or gratitude—that is, lessons that help your soul grow. After my husband, Larry, recovered from his benign brain tumor, he felt the ordeal helped him learn to live more in the moment, really cherish our family, and never put off anything he wants to do, whether it's riding his motorcycle on a whim or taking chances on a new business idea.

I also feel that emotional upsets, traumas, and losses—including those we experience from grief—can contribute to poor health. And often, to repair the health issue, it helps to recognize this and heal from whatever brought you down in the first place. I'm no doctor, but I've met a lot of people with health concerns like hernias, addictions, and fibromyalgia who were prompted or fed by anxiety, anger, sadness, and other negative emotions. For them, working through their issues helped their bodies accept healing from whatever source they used, whether it was medicine, surgery, healers, acupuncture, what have you. Their immune systems could actually focus on fighting their conditions without the additional, stress-induced symptoms.

From a spiritual point of view, I was taught that many of us are given option points where you have the opportunity to learn a lesson or change something about yourself for the better, which can result in healing the body. Many times, if you can recognize and release pain, or allow yourself to forgive a hurtful situation, an illness can turn around. Or, you may not be willing to let go of an upset or seek the right treatment, and that can cause you to get worse or lead to your passing. For example, during a private reading, Spirit told me that a woman's brother had terrible diabetes and that he might need to have a toe amputated. They said it was correctable, but he had to take certain steps to initiate healing. You could argue that this message was his "option point."

I love how Spirit gives advice but then leaves it to you to make wise, freewill decisions. No matter how great your life is, I think you'll always have regrets, so Spirit wants you to make as many informed choices as you can—particularly with your health, since you can carry emotional or physical illnesses into a future life. And even though the time that we're meant to pass is generally predetermined, destiny is not an excuse to eat junk food, become a dumpy old couch potato, or take thoughtless risks like skydiving without a parachute. The whole reason we're here in this world is to learn from our experiences. So you can choose not to take care of yourself and not learn your lessons and end up with sickness, pain, and unhappiness, but this would be counterproductive to your purpose, because you would set yourself up for suffering. Or, you can lead a happy, healthy, and productive life, as well as spiritually evolve in the time frame that has been designated and allowed for soul growth. I know which option I prefer!

To that end, it doesn't make much sense to blame God for "taking a life too soon." It's not like He arbitrarily swats out an otherwise healthy and happy existence, as if He's wielding one of those insect zappers that look like tennis rackets. Remember, your death is an agreed-upon choice between your soul, your guides, and God. It doesn't matter if the person who dies was good, pious, or a role model; in most cases, Spirit tells me that death happens when that particular soul, *not the human*, chooses to leave—even if the soul fights to stay when it's his time to cross over. I'm told that this is also the case with children who get sick or die young. Their souls have agreed to take on illnesses for the sake of their growth or for the loved ones connected to them. I once read a father who wanted his son to be a great baseball player, but the boy developed leukemia that didn't allow him to do all that this man expected of him. The child died from the cancer, and during a reading, his soul stepped forward to say that Dad was meant to learn about expectations and unconditional love from the limitations that his son's soul took on.

My cousin Keith and his wife, Meagan, are also learning from their child's challenges. They have two daughters, but miscarried a son at eight weeks. When Meagan got pregnant again with their daughter Alexa, they were overjoyed, yet at eight weeks old she was diagnosed as blind in her left eye and with compromised vision in her right. While Alexa is the happiest baby, her condition has been stressful on her parents' marriage. Initially, Alexa had surgery and then doctor's appointments three days a week; now she's getting physical and vision therapy four days a week. With this situation, I sensed that the lesson linked to the little girl is for her parents—that despite their current struggles, she is teaching them to remember why they fell in love in the first place. They're also learning gratitude for their three beautiful children and the incredible support network they have. Incidentally, their oldest daughter, Sophia, has begun seeing the soul of a young boy, and rainbows in their living room and at bedtime. Spirit says this is the child they miscarried, and the rainbows mean there's light at the end of this tunnel.

Though God isn't really to "blame" for a death, getting angry at Him is a natural part of grieving, and He knows that. It doesn't offend Him, because He realizes that part of what humans do when they grieve is look for something or someone to hold responsible. If getting mad makes you feel better, okay. Know that He will be there when you're ready to pick up where you left off. God has broad shoulders, as they say. It reminds me of how I get annoyed at Larry or the kids, yet no matter how frustrated I can act, I'm never going to divorce him or walk out on the family. We share a strong bond that will always keep us connected. Similarly, when you're mad at God, you can stomp and yell at Him all you want, but you don't need to turn from your faith to make a point.

Grief: It Gets Easier, I Promise

There is a period of grieving that everyone must go through, and it may be the hardest thing you'll ever do. You might have lost more than a father, because Dad was also your best friend. A neighbor who passed may have been the sister you never had. You can also suffer the impact of what that person has left you to do alone— cook meals, fill the gas tank, preset the thermostat, take care of the kids. You might feel shocked and numb, angry at everyone, ask a lot of "if only" and "what if" questions, slump around in a fog, and even wonder if it's worth going on. If that's not hard enough, you have to deal with inappropriate condolences, when all you want people to do is say they're sorry, offer assistance, drop off a casserole, and share a story about how your loved one touched their lives. And even then, it rarely helps, because you just want your husband or mother back, and nothing can be said or done to change that this won't happen. I get it, I get it, I get it.

As a medium, I've seen clients turn their lives around when they swallow three powerful points. First, that your departed loved ones are still interacting with you in this world, but in another form. Spirit's said to my clients, "I'm not sad, because I haven't lost anything. I'm still with you in a different way"—and that's very comforting. Second, that the soul made a decision to leave this life early for soul growth. And third, that you can learn to recognize when your loved ones are reaching out, so you can reach back.

There will always be a part of you that will grieve for the people you love, but Spirit assures me that healing isn't just possible, it's necessary. What might be harder to hear is that taking small steps to help in this process, each and every day, is a freewill choice. You'll grieve your loved ones for the rest of your life, but you can heal at the same time. My mom's done a lot of bereavement training to help her conduct support groups at our church and assist families with planning funeral masses, and she says many people don't know this. You may think that if you're feeling better, then that's a disloyalty to the person who passed. But you will always miss your loved ones, and they know that. Spirit's told me that they want you to embrace life without them.

Mom says that years alone won't heal the pain; what does is finding tools and people who can help you cope with your loss and put it in a different perspective. Eventually, it will feel okay to go out with friends again and let others be there for you. During Mom's training, she watched the teacher do an exercise that was very relatable. She said the instructor asked a woman to hold one bucket, while he carried another. He told the woman to put all the feelings she'd had while grieving into the pail—anger, loneliness, sadness, and others. Meanwhile, the man's bucket was full of sympathy, understanding, compassion, and other resources he could use to help her feel better. But, he said, her bucket was so full, for so long, that she couldn't make room for any of his tools. As time went on and the woman healed from some of the emotions in her bucket, she found space for what he could offer. I really liked this metaphor, and it reminds me of why support and bereavement groups are so useful when you're having a hard time. They give you the information, advice, and resources to work through your grief. They let you share your struggles with people who know how full or empty your bucket can be.

I want you to know that you're not alone in how you feel. Personally, I grieve my deceased loved ones every day. When Gram died, I cried all the time—when I was by myself in the car or saw a picture of her in an album or on my mantel . . . But on our first Christmas without Gram, I took steps to accept her passing and honor her memory. When I set the table, I put Gram's picture in an angel frame at the place where she usually sat. The photo was taken two weeks before she died, and Gram looks happy and beautiful. During dinner, we talked to that picture as if it were her. At one point, Mom was like, "Hey, Gram, how'd the meatballs turn out?" It gave everyone at the table permission to say her name, miss her together, and acknowledge that she will always be part of our family. It helped us normalize her absence and recognize that she will never be forgotten.

Don't Worry! They All Feel Fine!

As my clients grieve, I often find it interesting to hear that their biggest concerns aren't for themselves but about what the person who's passed on is feeling. *Is my wife experiencing the same sadness that I am? Does my child feel scared or lonely in Heaven?* I've had clients tell me that they devote hours to feverish prayer to make sure that their loved ones are safe and happy in Heaven, because they're sure that the soul must be as miserable as they are. But again, I remind them that souls don't experience the same heartache we do, because they're still with us and know they'll see us again. I also reassure them that their souls were greeted by familiar faces, and the reunion was joyful.

Often accompanying this emotional fear is a worry that the person physically suffered during their final moments on earth—because to us, death can look and sound really terrible. But Spirit promises that what you witness and hear during those final breaths is simply the body shutting down. From the initial moment that a life begins to end, be it the first pang of a heart attack or gunshot from a murder, the soul exits the body and no further suffering occurs. The soul leaves this world with dignity and grace. You know how on old soap operas, an actor would see bright, white headlights from a car coming toward *them,* and then *boom!*, the show would end? That's my symbol for when a person didn't know what was happening, they passed instantly, and there was no pain or suffering when they crossed. This comes up a lot with car accidents. One time, I channeled a girl who was walking on the highway, got hit by a car, and then her body was run over by other vehicles and tractor trailers. Her family imagined her lying on the pavement, suffering, as her body received repeated blows. But her soul said, "I know what you saw when you identified my body, but my soul had left." I remember another man who was hit by a car and dragged, and his soul said that he too died instantly and did not suffer.

Souls also remain unaffected in the bodies of those with Alzheimer's, dementia, and in a coma or vegetative state. With Alzheimer's or dementia, Spirit tells me that what you're witnessing isn't a soul that's suffering but one that's struggling against the limitations of the physical body. Spirit's said that comas and vegetative states, on the other hand, can occur when it is not the soul's destined time to leave this world, so these souls will simply live out the rest of their time in this way, if they don't recover. But here, the soul is also fine. In fact, I've channeled souls in these states, because it's like the body is asleep, and the soul has all the energy in the world. The most poignant time this happened was when I read a woman whose parents lived together in an assisted living facility. They were very ill for years, and the father took care of the mother, who had very bad dementia or Alzheimer's—ironically, I can't remember which. As these situations often go, it was the caretaker, the father, who died first, and the ill mother was still alive but unable to communicate very well. During the reading, I channeled the father, who said to his daughter, "I've been sitting at the end of your mother's bed, calling her for weeks. But she doesn't come. She's so stubborn!" And then I heard *the mother's* soul chime in, "I'm not stubborn! I'm just not ready to go!" The two went back and forth like this for a while, even though the mom wasn't dead. But as they carried on, I could feel that the mother was growing increasingly at peace with the idea of crossing over. "Don't worry," the father's soul finally assured his daughter. "When Mom passes, my soul will be there to greet her." Do you know, four hours later, the mom died? Incredible.

And while we're on the subject of bodily concerns, I want to cover one more. Clients ask me what happens to a soul if a body isn't recovered from a tragedy or is unable to be laid to rest for some reason. So in these cases, their soul is still at peace, because our bodies are just a shell. In fact, graveyards are for us, not your loved ones. It's where you go to remember them, but you can also do that from a mountaintop or your living room—they're around because of you. Same thing if Spirit shows up at their own funeral, which they often do. But they come because you are there. And if you have a reading, they might even validate their attendance by describing what their casket looked like, who showed up, if you fixed their hair, and what they wore when they were laid to rest— from hockey uniforms, to leather jackets, to Juicy Couture sweat suits. One time, a soul even told me he was buried in Timberland boots. Who still wears those?

Lending a Healing Hand

When you're mourning a person's death, it's very common to realize how brief and precious your own life is. You might start to care more about your health and see a nutritionist, take vitamins, hit the gym, try alternative medicine . . . Know that as you do, your loved ones are not personally capable of healing you or improving your health, unless they had those abilities in the physical world. Only God's energy can bring healing through prayer or a spiritual healer, and this requires faith and concentrated focus. I also believe that you can move the process along by changing the way you think, raising your vibration, and having faith in a power higher than yourself.

What your loved ones *can* do is look out for you and steer you to the right people or circumstances that lead to good health, if you specifically ask them to. They can put the right doctor or friend in your path, someone who'll know exactly what you need to feel better. I know a woman who prayed to her grandma while suffering from a painful pelvic condition, and the next morning, got an email from an old friend who randomly mentioned a surgeon who finally brought her relief. I also believe Nanny and Gram have intervened for our family's health on many occasions, but the time Gram helped heal Victoria from a gymnastics injury is one of my favorite stories ever.

During November of her junior year of high school, Vic tore the ACL, MCL, and meniscus in her left knee. Doctors call this injury "the unhappy triad," since it takes so long to recover from the cumulative damage. Not only did Victoria have to sit out all of her normal competitions, but colleges couldn't scout her, and she needed to commit to a school that fall. This added even more stress to the situation. My brother, a sports physical therapist, suggested Victoria see a specialist who, rather than do ASAP surgery like most doctors advise, told her that he had to reconstruct her ACL, but the MCL had the ability to heal on its own. The meniscus, meanwhile, was a real mess, and he wouldn't know what to do with that until he operated. We happened to schedule Victoria's surgery for January 6, or Little Christmas—an Irish holiday that celebrates the end of the season; it's also known as the Feast of the Epiphany, a Christian feast day that celebrates Jesus's physical presence as God's son. I, of course, took all of this to be a major sign. It gave my brother Michael time to rehab Victoria for two hours a day, five days a week; it gave Pat time to do a healing; and it gave Gram time to elbow God about doing His thing and help guide the process for everyone here as well.

On the morning of the surgery, our family was both confident and nervous. And after only an hour in the OR, the doctor said he was finished because all he had to do was reconstruct the ACL. What the huh? The MCL was healing, and the meniscus had re-attached itself and was back to normal. Not long after, we went back for her first checkup and the doctor showed us where he reinforced one side of the ACL with a screw, and the other with a button. A button! I know doctors do this, but it was a reassuring sign for us since Gram was a seamstress and collected buttons, and now there's a button sewn to my daughter's knee. I knew this was Gram's way of telling the family that she'd had a hand in Victoria's healing, sort of like how Zorro leaves his mark—Z—when he's saving the day. I should *also* mention that when I was telling this story to my cowriter Kristina, and we got to the button part, the lights dimmed in the room. We laughed for a minute, and when I said, "Gram, I like the lights better on!" they went back on. I then looked at the clock and it was 6:09 p.m. and 6/09 is the date Gram died. Talk about validation.

Another thing your loved ones can do from Heaven is warn you about health or safety scares, though I allow this in a reading only if a warning can prevent a bad situation or bring us comfort later. Many times with my clients' health, Spirit will guide them to healing by having me do what's called a "body scan." This is where I look at the person's external body and assess places on the inside that might need medical attention. If I see red spots in a given area, they are my symbol for cancers and severe illnesses that aren't being addressed properly or need to be approached differently; they can also mean that a person's holding on to negative emotions or situations, so I ask Spirit for ideas that can fix this. When I see pink spots, it means the person has a condition that isn't life threatening, and Spirit is already doing everything they can to help resolve it. They can also signify a benign situation like a food allergy that you will be able to rectify on your own.

What's clever is that there've been times when a person is very sick, but I don't see a thing because either Spirit's already doing everything they can to heal it and/or the client has decided there's nothing more to do. I once read a woman with stage-four cancer, but I saw no dots at all. Sure enough, the woman said the doctors had done everything they could, and she'd chosen to live the rest of her life without further medical treatment. I also read a man with pancreatic cancer who, to look at him, was hardly the picture of good health. But again, he had no issues when I did a body scan, though this time, it was because Spirit told me that he would soon be in full remission. He called me a few months later to confirm that his doctors told him he officially was.

Spirit also likes to warn clients about safety concerns, though not always in ways I expect. During a private reading for a mother, Spirit was very specific about the type of car her son drove. They told me his full name and said he never wears a seat belt. "I tell him every day to do that!" she huffed. The woman told her son about the reading, because we thought they might be warning him against a future injury. But shortly after the reading, the boy was killed in a car accident. His seat belt was off, but only because he momentarily unsnapped it to pick up an item that fell to the floor.

The reason, then, that Spirit told us about the seat belt was so the mom didn't torture herself after her son's death, wondering if she could have helped him prevent it. Another time, Spirit told me that a woman's daughter was pregnant, though the mom insisted this wasn't the case, because the girl was sixteen years old and not sexually active. I thought maybe I was wrong, but four months later, she called to say her daughter was going to have a baby, but she handled the news so well because I'd already told her about it. I feel Spirit revealed this news early so she'd support her daughter in a way she might not have if it were a surprise.

Healing: Do What You Can to Keep Going

When Spirit leads us to healing, I'm always impressed, because if you've ever chased answers with doctors about a tough health issue, they don't always give you the right answers at first! But when a client tells me that they've healed *emotionally* after a reading, I'm even more in awe because this is subjective. You can't see an emotional scar disappear, the way you can with a physical one. Yet time and again, the heartfelt healing that Spirit brings, often through a reading, is more powerful than years of therapy. And I say that as a woman who really respects therapists!

In chapter four, I mentioned my friend Geeta, who's an aesthetician and Reiki Master. (No, she doesn't do both at the same time. But how amazing would it be if she got rid of your depression while also waxing your upper lip?) Throughout her life, Geeta felt Spirit was sending her signs and messages, though she never really knew how to interpret them, how they related to her purpose, or what lessons she was supposed to learn from this lifetime. Like once, when she lived in Trinidad, she went to a temple to pray, and the steel *trishul*—a three-pronged spear that's cemented in concrete—began "shaking like a leaf in the wind," she said. Yet when Geeta lightly touched it, the movement stopped. Seeing a sturdy structure tremble for no reason would be enough for me to suspect it's an act of God or Spirit, but Geeta has since found an even deeper significance in it. She says traditionally, a *trishul* is a weapon used to destroy negativity, and this one was on the right side of the *lingam,* a stylized phallus worshipped as a symbol of the god Shiva. "The right hand is usually used to bless someone, so I believe I received blessings from the universe, destroying all negative energy, which began to allow good things to flow into my life, though I didn't fully realize it at the time," she said. The *trishul* shook for two more Sundays, and then three weeks later she moved to New York City, where things gradually changed for her in a very positive way.

She's since had many visitations while sleeping about her father, mother, and brother who'd died. One was about accepting things that made her uncomfortable, and four weeks after that, her husband passed away. She also had a dream that she was at the gates of Heaven and her aunt, who'd died a day earlier, told her to go back to earth and tell everyone that she was at peace. Geeta's seen Spirit in the form of light, like orbs on family photos and little flashing twinkles on the ceiling of the spa where she works. She thought this last one was a reflection from her jewelry, but when she shut off all the lights, they were still there.

When I met Geeta, she was in a very sad and stuck place from her husband's death, but after talking to her about Spirit and intuition for a year, I knew she had a gift worth honing that might also turn her mood around. I suggested she meet Pat, who introduced her to a Reiki Master we know. Geeta studied under her and has since healed others and herself. She's more positive and feels that her values are in line with who she is. She believes there is an infinite love connection that you have with your family that never dies and keeps you connected to them forever. Even more incredible is that her evolution has inspired her daughter Crystal to take Reiki classes as well, and though the two have a rocky past, they're close again. Her son Tyler feels his dad's presence and enjoys talking to Geeta about the emotions that connect us with the afterlife.

Another great example of a couple who received profound healing from a reading is one that I read in Zorn's, which is a skinless fried chicken place on Long Island. I did this on the show, but the curative effects happened after the cameras stopped rolling. The funny thing is, when I first walked in, there was a woman who recognized me and wanted a spontaneous reading so bad that she followed me everywhere. But Spirit pointed me to a couple who'd just left their son's basketball game and wanted chicken nuggets and fries to snack on before dinner.

The man's father had passed away three months prior to this, and it left the husband in a very dark place. He wasn't being social, he was drinking a lot, and he refused to go on vacation or simply enjoy himself around his adorable family. The guy had worked with his dad for thirteen years until he retired and then recently began a business similar to the one that his father owned. On weekends, the men went deep-sea fishing together, and they'd also talked about going on a Caribbean cruise with their families to celebrate the older man's eightieth birthday and the husband's fiftieth, which were a month apart. The father died before this could happen, so the family celebrated the father's birthday without him. When they did, they shared all the amazing signs they'd experienced since he died—lights turning on and off, a receipt from 1978 with the dad's signature found on the floor, pennies in odd places. The grieving son explained everything away. Even when the family found fifteen dollars in change in a parking lot, directly under their car, the man told his wife not to call it a sign. "You sound like a moron when you talk like that," he said. His dad kept trying to say he was around, but the son didn't see it. Until I met them at Zorn's.

I ran into this couple the day after the dad's eightieth birthday party. I told the husband that his father's soul said he was a good son and that he was very proud of him. Dad said he loved him very much and was in a better place. Though this impressed the wife, the husband looked hesitant and a little afraid. What I think clinched it for him was that the wife's grandmother's soul then stepped forward and validated her presence by telling us that as a child, the woman trained for the Olympics. She laughed, looked at me, and said, "I'm sixty pounds overweight! Do I look like an Olympian?"—so it's not like I could tell she was an athlete—but she *did* train to be an Olympic diver. As this happened, the woman got a whiff of Chanel #5 and cigarettes, her grandmother's signature scent. When the cameras were off, I pulled the wife aside and said, "Your father-in-law wants you to know that you saved his son." This blew her away, because the week he died, the man said to her verbatim, "I love you. You really saved my son." He was referring to how she helped her husband start his business back up again, after leaving his job a few years prior.

Before the reading, the husband's depression was very hard on his wife and family. But a week later, he snapped out of his funk. The kids got their father back, and he no longer drinks and retreats. He booked a fabulous trip to Cabo and told his wife, "I'm not mourning, because Dad is in a better place." And he meant it! He now believes that your soul lives on, and the family makes decisions knowing that Dad's with them and protecting them from the Other Side. "His whole way of seeing life changed overnight," the wife said later. "And it only cost us five dollars and sixteen cents for those nuggets and fries!"

Amazing stories like these can feel so rewarding, but they can also make it hard for me to do my job. They affect me so much! Usually I'm able to set aside my sentiments when I do a reading, because I take on the feelings and emotions of the soul communicating with me. Plus, who wants to see a mushy medium that's crying the whole time? But sometimes, I can't help myself. Not when your loved ones tell me how much the experience means to you and how huge it is in helping you move on.

One session where I struggled to keep it together was for a woman named Melanie. When I channeled her husband, Leon, I was moved to tears by their connection. The man died after cutting his foot on an anchor that was buried in a man-made lake near the Gulf of Mexico, despite being put on antibiotics for the infection. Prior to seeing me, Melanie regularly got signs that her husband's soul was near. For example, she kept seeing the number sixty-seven, which was the number on his football jersey when he played for Northwestern, and she saw his apparition lying next to her in bed one night but didn't tell anyone about it. During the reading, Spirit gave her the gift of healing by confirming that every sign she experienced was real and it was Leon reaching out. Spirit then let me trade places with Leon's soul. I'd never soul traveled before, so let me just say, it was *wild*.

As I channeled Leon, my soul floated above our session and looked down at my body interacting with Melanie. At the same time, Leon's soul was in my body, so when I was talking to her, I was mostly speaking as her husband. I kept getting confused about who was who, but Leon's soul made a lot of clear points. He said that certain sounds that his body made as he died were actually his soul trying to come back to earth, which is something his wife wondered about. I also validated that at his wake, she whispered an inside joke to him about his hair color. His soul talked about a memorial tree that his mother planted by a swing set, and he bragged that his favorite color was purple ("Real men wear purple," he told me). His soul also alluded to a teddy bear made out of his clothes, which was a double validation. Not only did Melanie take her oldest son to Build-A-Bear to make a football bear in Dad's honor, but her mom's friend said that she was secretly making three bears for Melanie's kids from scraps of Leon's clothes! As Leon, one of the last things I told Melanie was, "I want you to know that you will love again, and I'm going to handpick somebody to love you and be there for our children." Melanie later confided to me that at the end of long, hard days, she talked to Leon aloud about how terrified she felt spending the rest of her life as a single mother. Then she'd feel guilty for thinking this. But after the session, she knew Leon was addressing her concerns, because he knew this was his big chance to tell her what she needed to hear.

Perhaps most incredible of all was what happened the morning of Leon's funeral. Melanie woke up feeling nauseous and wondered if she could be pregnant. She took four tests and all of them confirmed that she was. Melanie was five months along and showing when I met her, but I knew that she was four weeks pregnant when she found out. I also knew she'd be giving birth to a boy. Leon's soul told me that she'd see his traits in their child and to look for a birthmark to show that he held the baby's soul prior to coming here. He then said that if she doesn't sense or see Leon anymore, this means that his soul was reborn in her child. "Either way, the minute you hold him, you will feel that something is different about this baby," I said. She told me that she plans to give the child the middle name of Leon. "I don't doubt that God gave me this baby for comfort," she said to me. "It is just one more reason to put my feet on the ground every day."

The day after I channeled Leon, I received an email from Melanie that makes me grateful for my gift and its ability to alleviate grief and usher in healing. It reminds me why I am so amazed by Spirit every day. Here are some lines from her note:

There are not enough words to thank you for making yesterday a reality for me. From the second Leon died, my entire world stopped moving. I lost all hope, faith, and comfort. There wasn't a day that went by that I didn't pray that somehow, some way, I would be awarded the chance to [connect with him again] . . . *Through my experience and reading, I now know without a doubt that Leon is with me, more now than ever before . . . Leon was my life. I had felt as if I would never feel happiness again, never have any peace with where my life is at. I am different today, because of Theresa and her team awarding me this opportunity. I haven't slept since the night Leon died, but I slept like a baby last night. I woke up today, and my heart wasn't as heavy. I woke up today knowing that Leon is right here with me and our boys. I woke up today finally believing that I'm going to be OK . . . You have no idea what this has done for me, my family, and my children. I will forever be the person and mother I was meant to be because of you. Because now I can allow it. You've changed my life, and . . . I thank you from the bottom of my heart.*

Believe me, I will never forget Melanie or her husband's generous soul. Oh no, here I go again . . . Somebody pass the tissues!

10

Spirit Gets the Final Say

I'm not exactly bashful when it comes to saying what's on my mind. I like to talk, and if you ask me about food, family, or any of the Kardashians, you'll learn that I have opinions to spare. I sometimes wonder if the fact that I like to yammer on is the reason that God gave me this gift; maybe He knew I'd never run out of breath when delivering Spirit's messages! And while I think *I* have a lot to say, your deceased loved ones have me beat. When Spirit channels through me, they can be an impressively talkative bunch.

As you've learned, Spirit is big on offering words that bring comfort, peace, direction, and validation that they're with you. And I think they do this because you're constantly telling them, in your thoughts and prayers, how much you miss them and wish they were around. So by reassuring you through a reading or showing you signs in your own life, I feel that's their way of answering your needs and requests. But I've *also* noticed that tucked within their main messages of healing and validation are much subtler, secondary meanings that I might not recognize in the moment.

It makes sense to me that Spirit's thoughts would be significant from a few angles, because so many things in life are. When have you read a book, had a conversation, heard a story, or watched a movie . . . and gotten only one message from it? Our experiences in the physical world are too nuanced for that. Also, not everyone comes to see me when they're sad, so Spirit's communication can't only be about coping with grief. Some people come for readings because they want to catch up with their loved ones or receive validation that they're on the right track. But no matter what Spirit wants you to mainly know, there are usually more layers to what they're saying than we realize.

So in closing, I want to leave you with ten incredible lessons I've learned from channeling Spirit all these years. Some of these were the driving points of the messages I delivered, but many were the poignant undertones that rang true to me. I hope they resonate with you on many levels too, no matter where you are in your life.

#1: The little things that matter to you still matter to your loved ones.

When Spirit validates their presence with specific references that I couldn't possibly know, this doesn't just tell you that their existence is "real." It also shows you that no matter how busy your loved ones are in Heaven, they're never too preoccupied to forget the moments and memories that made their lives in the physical world with you so special. For example, when I did a show in Orlando, I read a woman whose husband drowned in a lake. He was athletic and knew how to swim, which made his death hard to understand, but his soul had predetermined that it was his time to pass on.

As I channeled, the man's soul came through to confirm that he's still around by recognizing that the wife is making a quilt in his memory from green army fatigues, and that on the car ride over, her daughter was talking to her about becoming a specials-needs teacher.

These validations were sweet, but they were nothing compared to what happened next. His soul then showed me a body of water and a dinghy, which I thought referenced how he died, by drowning in a lake. But his wife's friend corrected me. "Dinghy was *my* husband's nickname for me. He also died," she explained. "Our husbands were best friends." The man who drowned then brought his best friend's soul forward; they were together on the Other Side. The fact that Dinghy's husband remembered her pet name, and then reminded his friend's soul of it so that he could connect with her, made me smile. It's these special, inside references—from private jokes, to personal conversations, to instances you remember when you're alone—that will never stop mattering to your loved ones even after they've passed, because they're still important to you.

Another story that demonstrates Spirit's enduring attention to detail happened during a fund-raiser for Victoria's gymnastics team. I felt a soul tap me on the shoulder and say, "Can you please tell my wife how beautiful she is? She's wearing a blue shirt." I turned around to find a woman standing behind me in a blue shirt, so I asked her, "Did you lose your husband?" She did. "He wants you to know how beautiful you are," I said. Of course, everyone in the room was like, *Aww, that's so sweet.* But after the event, the woman told me her husband's message had a second layer to it. "I was married to him for over twenty-five years before he died," she said. "I just started dating again, and on the way here, I said to my daughter, 'I hope Daddy isn't upset that I'm dating, because what I really love about my new companion is that every day, he tells me how beautiful I am. In twenty-five years, your father never did that.'" But at that fund-raiser, his soul finally did. And by telling the wife that she is beautiful, the man's soul gave her what she needed to hear to calm her worries and change the way she potentially saw her new relationship. She wasn't just replacing her husband with a new man but living her life as a woman who was loved and will be loved again. And to my original point, Spirit's message addressed a very private, specific, and persistent sentiment that was an undercurrent throughout the couple's marriage. I always say, I don't have to identify with the message, and I don't care if anybody else gets it, so long as the person that Spirit is speaking to appreciates it.

#2: Don't doubt when your loved ones are trying to connect.

Everyone connects to their loved ones differently, and you don't have to be a medium to know that some signs like flickering lights or apparitions in your bedroom are easier to recognize than others. But as you know, seeing a soul in a dream can be a means of connecting that you're not so sure about the next day. Is it your dead sister's soul if she was dressed as Cleopatra? Did your son's spirit visit you in a dream, even if he was babbling about the Red Sox and not giving you a heartfelt message? The whole debate reminds me of that old saying: *If a soul appears in a dream, and there's no medium around to validate it, did it really happen?* But I did the best reading where Spirit told me that random dream appearances can be a way of connecting, and the soul is with you at that moment.

Here, I channeled a young man who died from using drugs that worsened an existing heart condition. The small room was full of close family and friends. I gleaned from his messages that some of the guests were connecting with him very easily, and others weren't. He then told me about a girl there who dreamed of him kneeling down in front of her and asking her to marry him. The two were best friends and not romantic—so for all intents and purposes, this just seemed like a nonsensical dream to her. But his soul intently stepped forward to say that he was connecting with her that night in her silly dream, though he clearly wasn't proposing marriage in the afterlife. Then his soul actually kneeled down in front of me, the way that he did for her, to validate it. What a romantic!

#3: The dead never need to RSVP.

Spirit looks forward to a big event as much as you do. Reunions, vacations, weddings, graduations—your loved ones are with you, at all of them, in spirit. When I channeled the soul of a man who committed suicide, though he had a few lessons to learn on the Other Side, he said he still made time to fuss with the microphone at his sister's wedding. I also read an entire family whose loved one stepped forward to say that the soul planned to attend a kindergarten graduation and validated it by showing that the little girl would be wearing her hair in braids. And if Spirit attends your child's birth, who knows? They may bring your pets along! At a bingo hall in Long Island, I read a woman whose mom died almost twenty years ago. When she was alive, the daughter was told she couldn't have kids, so she got a black Lab named Sammy. After Mom died, she proved her doctors wrong, had a baby, and always wondered if her mom knew about it. Her dog had also recently passed. During the reading, the mother's soul stepped forward to say that she knew all about her beautiful granddaughter and that Sammy, the Lab, was with her in Heaven.

#4: They can hear you talking to yourself.

Souls communicate through thought, so when you want to talk to your deceased loved ones, you don't have to put on a show to get their attention. You don't even need to speak out loud. You can silently communicate to Spirit and God with your thoughts and the feelings you project, and they'll hear you. At a fund-raiser for the Boys and Girls Club in Hicksville, I did a reading for three siblings, two girls and a boy. Their ages ranged from early teens to early twenties, yet they'd lost both their parents already. When I channeled the parents' souls, they did some cute validations. Dad kept telling me, "John-John"—which was the father's name and the name of the son. The young man was also wearing his dad's bracelet with the name John on it, and the family lived on John Street. Mom, who died almost a decade earlier, also verified her presence by reminding her youngest daughter how they used to rub their fingers on a yellow blanket with satin trim. But what really spoke to me was when the mother's soul said to the girl, "I know how hard you try to remember my voice or feel me holding you. Know that I'm with you when you think about this." Mom wasn't just telling her that her soul is around when she needs it, but that she could feel the energy of her daughter's thoughts. That was enough to get her attention.

Similarly, I know a woman who lost her husband when he was thirty-three years old, and two years after he passed, she was in a real funk around the holidays. She hadn't prayed for a sign in a while, but her husband's soul still knew that she needed a pick-me-up. One day on her way to work, she got stuck in traffic and noticed that the car in front of her had two bumper stickers. One was for the New York Jets, her husband's favorite team, and the other said "Live, Laugh, Love," which is what he'd had engraved on the inside of her wedding band. When she saw the pairing, she laughed for the first time in months. "He must have known what a mood I was in, because he really hit me over the head with these signs," she told me. "There is no question that he was saying that he loved me, was with me, and was doing all he could to help me, and I didn't even have to ask."

#5: Spirit doesn't want you to know *everything*.

When you find yourself in a confusing or challenging situation, it's good to turn to God, souls of faith, or loved ones for answers. But if you don't get one, it can be really confusing. When this happens to me, I've admittedly thought, *What's the point of having connections up there, if nobody's listening?* But then I remember that Spirit tells clients that just because their prayers aren't always answered, it doesn't mean they're not heard. The hard truth is, the outcome of a situation may not be changeable or a frustration may be meant to teach a lesson to you or someone in your life. But you don't know this at the time, so you react by feeling alone, abandoned, or really frigging mad.

There are also topics that Spirit simply doesn't discuss. Some mediums welcome questions either throughout or at the end of a session, but if at any time a client says he or she wants to ask me something, I first ask Spirit to give me a "yes" or "no" before the person even finishes his or her sentence—and only if it's a "yes" will

I entertain it. If I get a "no" from Spirit, that's my sign that they aren't concerned with the answer or that the response is one that we're not ready to hear or that your loved one isn't ready to communicate. For instance, Spirit has never been too keen on talking about the impending death of a person who's alive. They also don't love to get specific about the year or time that an event might happen, since it has the potential to alter how you'll live your life until then. Spirit might volunteer a month, but that could mean this year or five years from now, and that's a timeline they manage to keep vague. I know a woman who saw two well-known mediums, both of whom told her she'd buy a new home in June, and both felt it would happen that year. The woman and her family were so excited and counted down until then, but June came and went without a new place. I don't know if these mediums were wrong or if Spirit meant June of a different year. What may have happened is that they were given the feeling of it happening "soon," but that's a subjective sensation. If Spirit makes me feel that an event happened "recently," that means within two years. A two-year difference to a soul means nothing because in the grand scope of eternity, it isn't a long time. But to a family hoping to move or grieving a loss, two years can feel like forever! So I've made peace with the fact that time doesn't have meaning on the Other Side. We use clocks and calendars to make schedules and give our lives order, but Spirit doesn't have deadlines or eighty-three errands to run by five p.m.

#6: Most of Spirit's messages are for you, and only you.

Although Spirit piggybacks messages in a large group and viewers have emailed me to say that a reading on TV resonated with them, it amazes me that Spirit's communication is usually really specific. The best example of this is when I channeled the same soul for two sisters, in back-to-back readings. I didn't realize they were related when I booked them, because I don't ask for last names. But when I channeled the first woman's father, his soul gave me a message and said, "That's for the *next* reading." The other sister was waiting in the car, and I had no idea. So when the second woman came in for her session, I asked how she knew the person before her. "I feel a father figure hanging around," I said, "and I'm not sure why he's still here. Usually Spirit leaves when you do." That's when I found out that the two women were related, and the only thing these sisters had in common was the person they lost. Their father's messages were different because the women have different needs, and those are what his soul specifically addressed.

#7: Cherish your loved ones' memory, not their booty.

It's no secret that people tend to get a little grabby when a loved one dies. *I'll take the Venetian mirror! I want the cordial glasses! Dibs on the cocktail ring!* The point of inheriting a prized possession is to have an item that reminds you of your family member or friend, not to acquire a piece that gets you on *Antiques Roadshow*. When Nanny died, it's surprising that she came to me as a big, fat fly instead of as a big, fat diamond because the woman had a lot of gorgeous gems. When we divvied up her stuff, one family member got a stunning ring, another got a fancy bracelet . . . and I was given her simple, gold cross. Though I was only sixteen years old at the time, I won't lie—I felt slighted. I know that sounds shallow, but it's true. Then about fourteen years later, on Christmas morning, Nanny came to me and said, "You have my most precious piece of jewelry." I don't know the history of her cross, or why it meant so much to her, but I began to treasure it more after that. The cross wasn't her most expensive possession, but it was one of her most valuable pieces. Her visit also came when I was building my library of signs and symbols, so whenever Spirit shows me Nanny's cross, it means that a soul wants to talk about how a person has *their* most precious piece—be it a quilt, journal, scarf, you name it. And surprise, surprise, the meaning that Spirit attaches to their most cherished items usually outweighs their monetary value.

#8: Don't waste energy on survivor's guilt.

This subject is important to Spirit, mostly because survivor's guilt keeps you from embracing life without your loved ones, which is the opposite of what they want you to do. One of the most amazing times that this came up was when I read a woman on the show who had stage-four breast cancer and her sister-in-law died from the same disease when it was only in stage one. The two women bravely fought their condition together, and the one who is still here felt tremendous survivor's guilt for outliving her sister-in-law and also for all the energy that her friends and family devoted to helping her feel well, when in retrospect, she wondered if her relative needed it more. Another time, I channeled the soul of a girl who'd asked her friend to pick her up from a party, but it was late at night, and she was tired, so she asked her pal to grab a cab or find another ride. When she did, the car crashed and the girl died. You can imagine the guilt her friend had for not dragging herself out of bed to pick up her friend from the event. But her soul told us that even if the friend had picked her up, they still would have had an accident, and then the girl would have also felt guilty about contributing to her death. She wouldn't have saved her friend's life. In both situations, Spirit wanted these people to release any survivor's guilt they felt connected to the passing and try to move forward. The recurring thoughts, images, and dreams that people experience when they suffer from survivor's guilt can be torturous and haunting for them, and your deceased loved ones don't want you to experience these feelings. They want you to release this burden, and recognize that you still have a lot to do and appreciate here in the physical world.

#9: Don't take your life for granted.

I will never tell people who are grieving a loss that they need to move on already. But Spirit does want you to embrace your life without your loved ones, if just in baby steps—first in moments, then days, then entire months . . . as best you can. During a show in Tampa, a boy's soul came through to say that two weeks prior, he died from what was ruled a suicide but was truly a homicide. He was shot point-blank in the chest by a shotgun, which, he reminded me, is nearly impossible unless you have Go-Go Gadget arms. He showed me that his mother was in a dark and heavily medicated place, and his soul validated its presence by saying that Mom had his car deed with her (she then pulled it out of her purse) and that he supports how she's laying him to rest (she'd made the decision the day before). And though this concerned soul was trying so hard to say, "Look, Ma, it's me. I'm okay," the mom told me that all she saw was despair.

What the boy's soul said next, however, did resonate with her in a significant way. He told her that he knows that she prays to fall asleep and never wake up, but that it is not her time to die, and she needs to stay in this world for a while without him. "I was all my mother had," he told me, as an explanation for her crippling grief. He went on to say that she doesn't need to take her life to be with her son, because he is with her every time she feels sad and misses him. Equally startling, perhaps, is that the woman was invited to my show at the last minute by a friend with an extra ticket, so she easily could have missed this enormous message from her thoughtful and sympathetic son. I really feel that his soul's words opened his mom's eyes and possibly saved her life.

#10: Seize the day, not just Spirit.

I have a strong faith and know a lot about the Other Side, but Spirit doesn't run my life for me, and they won't do the same for you. They will intervene, assist, and guide you from Heaven, but the crux of your life is what *you* make of it. Thanks to free will, your decisions are what determine whether the majority of your time here is full of pleasure or despair, certainty or doubt, trust or skepticism. To pursue the most positive path, which is what I try to do every day, you really must choose to meditate, pray, visualize, let go of fear, be grateful, raise your vibration, and ultimately believe that God, other Spirit, and your loved ones are around you. Their presence means that your thoughts are heard, prayers are being answered, and that miracles can unfold. I have a lot of respect for Abe Lincoln, and I've always liked when he said, "And in the end, it's not the years in your life that count. It's the life in your years." I can only hope that my gift will continue to help you fill your years with faith, happiness, laughter, and an abundance of love.

Afterword

A Word from My Ghost— Er, Spirit—Writer

One of the most fun parts of my job as a cowriter is that I'm forced to get inside my author's head and understand what it's like to "be her," so that the story feels compelling and credible. This usually happens through interviews and over lunches, in a very natural and comfortable way. But when I initially thought about whether I could "be Theresa," I was a little concerned. I adored her from the very instant we met and was a big fan of her show, but I'm not from Long Island, I don't speak to dead people, and I haven't bought hair spray since 1984. How would I pull this off? Well, as you know from the book, Spirit is a literal and well-intentioned bunch, and my thoughts must have doubled as prayer. Let's just say that if I ever wrote a memoir about what my family went through as I worked on this project, I might have to call it *That Time We Were Psychic.*

I've always believed that mediums can connect with the Other Side, and for some, this gift comes from God; my husband, Scott, however, is another story. He was a real skeptic, and when I asked him how he thought I should handle the few, small details Theresa wasn't sure about, he joked, "Do what all mediums do. Make it up!" (Don't worry, we turned to Spirit and Pat for answers instead.) So it was pretty funny that when our household began experiencing Spirit, the souls went straight to Scott and not me. He began "seeing things," which challenged his beliefs, so you can only imagine how thrown and scared he felt at night. All told, Scott saw kids floating outside our second-floor bedroom window, a little girl beside the bed, a man in a suit and hat at the foot of it, and a white dress floating across the room. Once, he even sat up and began pointing to the corner of the room, but in a way that looked like his arm was being yanked. Scott woke me with each sighting, but he said the souls disappeared when he did. I was later told that these beings weren't attached to our house or property, but were coming around because of the book; they wanted to tell their stories. Because we all connect with Spirit differently, only Scott had the ability to see them. I said a quick prayer that these souls leave the poor guy alone, and the craziness stopped for him. Then, it began for me.

First, I experienced physical sensations in and out of bed. I'd close my eyes, and before drifting to sleep, I sensed what Pat later said was Spirit being close to my body. One night, I felt a prickly energy push against my back and heard a whooshing noise in both ears, as if I were underwater. Another time, shortly after I closed my eyes, I could see myself lying in bed, as if I were outside my body, and then I felt like the inside of me (my soul?) was being shaken; when I opened my eyes, my chest felt very heavy. Needless to say, I beat it out of bed, grabbed the dog, and made Scott come to sleep earlier than he wanted. And sometimes when I wrote, I heard a high-pitched ringing noise in my right ear, or it felt full or turned beet red and very hot. This sent me running to an ear, nose, and throat doctor, who said I was fine and had perfect hearing. As it turns out, these ear symptoms can occur when Spirit is nearby.

I shared some of my initial experiences with Theresa and Pat, who taught me how to establish boundaries and ground and protect myself, which we then put in the book. I did this every morning and night, before bed. I also saged the house twice a week. I never thought any of this was negative Spirit—just souls without boundaries, or at worst, a low-energy soul that had found its way in and was easy to smudge out. It all reminded me of how Theresa said she felt before she knew how to control the energy around her.

I also had very vivid experiences when I closed my eyes. Most of the time, I'd see faces. I had clear, realistic dreams as well, where I was put into different scenarios we'd planned to cover in the book. Life reviews. Reincarnation. My soul swiftly leaving my body after a brutal death. They were like brief, rapid, back-to-back movie scenes, and they'd crowd my sleep so intensely that I'd be exhausted the next morning. I prayed that they stop, and they did. They were then replaced by visitations from my loved ones, which I cherished. My favorite was from my uncle, who was on a tour bus with people I didn't know. He was wearing a Hawaiian shirt and had binoculars around his neck. The visitation lasted for seconds, as he looked at me and said, "I'm just passing through, but you need to know that what she says about lessons is real." And then I woke up. He was a clever storyteller and witty man. Clearly, he kept his quirky personality in Heaven.

During those initial weeks, I wondered if my imagination was running wild because I was so close to the material, but then our dog Izzy started to act strange. She barked and growled at the landing of our staircase, hid under my desk as I wrote, and stared calmly at the end of a bench in my office. In various rooms, her head darted around as if she were tracking a fast-moving object in the air. Her eyes grew really wide each time, and she'd look up at me like, "Did you *see* that?" It was so cute, but also super weird. When she jumped into my arms shaking at one point, I asked Spirit to please stop scaring her, and from then on, her head continued to look like it was watching invisible entities, but she no longer seemed afraid. She'd watch for a while, and then take a nap.

I had a theory about what was going on: Maybe I was experiencing the chapters as we did them. When we wrote about connecting with Spirit and recognizing signs, I experienced details related to the topic. My chest felt heavy, though an X-ray said I was fine, and when I was mentally obsessing over this, a truck with the words "Heaven's Best Carpet Cleaners" pulled up in front of me (I think I may have blocked energy in my chest like Theresa did before she knew how to channel it). Both in our house and once at a restaurant, teeny white feathers floated down from the ceiling, mere inches from my face. When I went on Google Maps to see how long it would take to drive to Theresa's house, I was told one hour and eleven minutes (111 is said to be a sign of, among other things, spiritual awakening and enlightenment). And in the middle of winter, a big, fat, hairy fly buzzed around my TV room, which I immediately assumed was Nanny. Scott tried to kill it with a magazine, but I refused to let him. After he swore that I'd officially lost my mind, he tucked me into bed, and when he went back in to watch TV, the fly was dead on his side of the sofa. It's like Nanny was saying, "Okay, my work here is done. I'm out."

As we went along, I also felt heightened emotions related to each chapter. I was deeply sad while writing about grief and broke out in scary, unexplainable hives when we talked about negativity. They appeared as weltlike scratches, and while the health nut in me knows that can happen if you have high histamine levels, it was eerie to see and new for me. Spirit was also quick to squash any hampering disbelief I might have had. One night I woke up around three a.m. to see little lights flashing over my dresser. I felt like my eyes were playing tricks on me, so I dismissed it. A few days later, I interviewed Theresa's friend Geeta, who told me, unprompted, that she saw the same thing years ago. She's intuitive, and for her, it was Spirit.

I didn't naïvely accept that every sign was from Spirit. When my dog growled and barked in the kitchen, I snooped around and found a mouse, not a soul. I also debunked a rag doll that fell off a shelf; at first, I thought Gram did this because it happened after writing an email about her, but then I realized that when I stepped on the area rug a certain way, it made the shelf move and the doll fall. Most coincidences, however, were indisputable. My favorite happened when I interviewed a woman named Melanie about her reading for the show. She told me that when she sees light stream through clouds, she calls them "God's rays" and considers it a greeting from her loved ones' souls, including her husband's. I wrote chapter nine on a dark, dismal day, but when I got to the part about Melanie, the brightest, warmest ray of light broke through the clouds and shone only on my hands as I typed. I don't get direct sun in my office, so this has never happened. And then there's the incident with the letter *S* on my computer. I initially spelled "Spirit" with a capital *S*, but decided halfway through the book that it should be lowercase. So I tried using the "find and replace all" function to change all "Spirit" to "spirit," but the document wouldn't make the adjustment. It would, however, change all "spirit" to "Spirit." Out of curiosity, I tried this with some other letters of the alphabet, and *S* was the only one that didn't work with this function. Okay, *S*pirit it was!

Such a sudden and unexpected flurry of Spirit in my life made me wonder if God was addressing my initial concern—that I wouldn't be able to convincingly "be Theresa." Because she feels things in a way that most of us don't, it was occasionally hard for her to describe her experiences. But when I felt them too, I had a baseline and examples to reference. Seeing and sensing also made it easy for me to believe in such an out-there project for me. I would never work on a book that I felt was deceptive or fake in any way.

Though all of my experiences felt so real to me, when I shared my stories with friends, I got a quick lesson in Skepticism 101. Most were on board, but some looked at me like I had four heads. So I rambled on for hours with believers, and shut my trap with cynics who made me feel embarrassed and dumb. I figured that this must be how mediums feel when they're grilled by doubters, because like Theresa, I eventually found myself thinking, *I don't even care if you buy this. I'm not here to convince you. I just want to share the astonishing things I've experienced.* Then I'd choose my audience more carefully the next time. Thank God my mom and sister couldn't get enough.

Once I felt comfortable with everything that was happening, my intuition shot through the roof. I occasionally had a "sense of knowing" that Theresa also has, and Scott began calling me "Ed Glosser: Trivial Psychic," based on the old *Saturday Night Live* sketch about a man whose ridiculous readings aren't very useful. I can't blame him. I offhandedly mentioned that I was surprised that our neighbor's chickens hadn't found their way into our yard yet, and the next morning, our yard was full of chickens. I also knew my friend Jenny was pregnant before she told anyone outside her family. When the dog jumped off the sofa and began limping, I held her ankle, prayed for healing, and her limp was gone. And the minute I stepped into an antique store with my friend Beth, I wanted butter cookies nestled in white ruffled cups, stored in an old-fashioned tin. I'd never had such a specific craving, but whatever. I told the cashier I'd skipped lunch and asked if she had anything sweet for my blood sugar. "I don't want you to faint! Here," she said, and pulled out an antique tin of butter cookies, white paper cups and all.

One of the cutest incidents for me, personally, was when the souls of my departed loved ones helped with the book. I didn't experience them in any "psychic" way, but when Theresa did, I got the chills. My Nana and cousin Mimi regularly stepped forward in interviews to demonstrate points that were tricky for Theresa to explain. If she needed to, say, illustrate how Spirit looked or moved through space, Mimi or Nana acted it out, so Theresa could describe it as it happened. At one point, I didn't get what Theresa meant about how souls look if they sit with a family member, so Nana did it for her in a way I could understand. I could easily imagine her saying, "For God's sake, Kristina. It's like *this*."

As the book came to a close, I could feel most of the energy leaving my house. It was subtle yet incredibly obvious at the same time. The best comparison I can make is when your home is really dusty, and you don't even realize it until after you vacuum and the air feels so much clearer and lighter. There was an energy that no-ticeably remained, though—whatever was on my bench—because it still captivated Izzy for hours.

When Theresa and I finished her book, she gave me a private reading. My Nana, Mimi, and Spirit guide—who appeared to her as a bright, angelic light—stepped forward. They confirmed what I'd suspected all along, and then some. "Your Nana wants you to know that what you were sensing was real," she said. "They made you feel what you were writing, so that you understood it. Your guide says they worked hand in hand with you, so the book would be effortless." She went on to clarify that when signs and symbols occurred, they were caused by Nana and Mimi but orchestrated by my awesome guide. She is the one who sat in my office every day, engaging my dog so intently.

I didn't share every spiritual moment I had with Theresa, so I think the extent of it caught her by surprise. "Wait, they're saying they allowed you to be me for a moment? What the hell?" She laughed. "It's funny, though, because I also feel there's a sense of apology for making you feel what you did, but you have to under-stand, that is my life."

Yes, I get it, I *know*. What I never imagined was that "being Theresa" would be such an incredible experience. Not only because I truly respect what she does, but also because her access to God and Spirit leave absolutely no room for doubt in my life. I received so much validation about God and the afterlife during this proj-ect that my faith in Him has grown tremendously, as has that of many friends. The book has impacted my marriage too. Scott now believes that your soul lives on, and he has a more active inter-est in God. When I recently heard him start a sentence with the words "God willing . . ." I nearly choked on my burrito. It's clear to us that positive and seemingly unbelievable things can happen to anyone, at any time, and they can change your life if you let them.

On a Saturday-afternoon drive to see Pat for a hive-related healing, Scott summed it up pretty nicely. "Marriage and life in general come with a lot of surprises," he said, "but I never thought you'd know a celebrity psychic, have a healer, and that I'd be the one shuttling you back and forth to see them." Neither did I, baby. Neither did I.

Acknowledgments

I couldn't have written this book without the love, encouragement, and guidance I've received throughout this process and as a medium—from people in the physical world and Spirit on the Other Side. I'm so appreciative of everyone who's helped me grow and learn, even if I'm also an airhead who might forget to mention you below.

My warmest thanks to my coauthor, Kristina Grish, for your hard work and dedication to understanding me and Spirit. Who knew that being trapped in a hotel room for twelve hours a day would be that much fun *and* create such an amazing book? I think the sticky buns helped! And to my editor, Johanna Castillo, and the entire team at Atria Books, for believing in me and turning this project into a reality. Johanna, I know you worked really hard to make this happen, and I'm so grateful that you did!

To my incredible manager, Courtney Mullin, who cemented this deal and has been with me from the start. I'm truly thankful for your direction, business savvy, good instincts, and long-term vision that always knows what's right for me. You shelter me from stressful situations, make sure I'm taken care of, and remind me to enjoy the ride. Also, to your sister Victoria Woods, for telling you that I was "made for television." I think she was onto something!

To Magilla Entertainment's Laura Palumbo Johnson, Brian Flanagan, and Matt Ostrom, who knew within five minutes that we had something special. To Jonathan Partridge, for putting your heart and soul into the show, and to our hardworking crew, for making it a blast to come to work every day in my own house. And to everyone at TLC, especially Joanna Brahim and Tara Patten, for supporting who I am and what I do.

I also want to thank the people who help take the show on the road, including Rich Super from Super Artists and everyone at Mills Entertainment, for making my live experiences a success. I'm grateful to the talented and generous Michele Emanuele for always helping me look fabulous, and to my attorney, Jeff Cohen, for having my best interests in mind.

To my sweet and calm assistant, Courtney White, for basically running my life. Thanks for being "Positive Polly" and always assuring me that everything will be okay.

To Pat Longo, for helping me grow my gift, always reminding me to stay grounded, and never letting me forget where I came from. Thank you for being there when I need you—morning, noon, and in the middle of the night. I'm really appreciative of all you did to help with this book too. We couldn't have done it without you.

To Eileen Bacchi, for putting up with all my anxieties before we knew what the heck was going on. E, you are a special friend, and I will always value our relationship. Nobody "takes the kids to the store" like we do—back and forth, back and forth . . .

To Desiree Simonelli, for renewing our friendship after so

many years, with no questions asked. I miss our Friday-night pizza parties! I am so glad you're in my life.

To Bill and Regina Murphy, for allowing Brian to be the first child I ever channeled. It was such an honor then, and I feel blessed that his soul is still around me.

To my big Italian family on both sides, including aunts, uncles, and cousins, particularly Aunt Debbie and Aunt Gina, for being such a big part of my world while I was growing up. And to my cousin Lisa Brigandi, whom I can talk to about anything and everything. You know, firsthand, what it is to walk in my shoes, and you do it gracefully.

To my parents, Ronnie and Nick, for being the best neighbors a girl could ask for, and for supporting me as I found my way in life. It couldn't have been easy to understand my abilities at first, but you had faith in me and I cherish that. And Dad, I know this freaks you out, but thank you for never questioning my intentions or sanity. I also want to thank my brother, Michael, and his family for accepting and supporting me. I'm always here for you and the kids, in case they take after Aunt Theresa (if you know what I mean)! To Gram and Nanny Brigandi, for guiding me when I started all of this and still visiting me when I need them the most. And to Connie, Jack, and the whole Caputo clan for loving me and giving me the best gift of all—your son.

To my husband, Larry, and the kids, for knowing when to give me a hard time and when to make me feel like a million. Larry, you are the love of my life, and I thank God every day that you fell for the perky girl with big hair. Larry Jr. and Victoria, thanks for putting up with the house always smelling like sage, when I know you wish it smelled like my meatballs with vodka sauce.

ACKNOWLEDGMENTS

Last but never least, I'm eternally thankful to God and Spirit for all the blessings in my life—foremost among them, my amazing clients and fans. Because of you, I've learned more about forgiveness, growth, and unconditional love than I ever knew was possible. Thank you for trusting me with your hearts and your loved ones' souls.

xoxo,

Theresa